YORK NOTES

General Editors: Professor A.N. Jeffares (*University of Stirling*) & Professor Suheil Bushrui (*American University of Beirut*)

Thomas Mann

TONIO KRÖGER

Notes by Colin Niven

MA (CAMBRIDGE)
Head of Modern Languages, Sherborne School

LONGMAN
YORK PRESS

Extracts from H.T. Lowe-Porter's translation of
Tonio Kröger by Thomas Mann are reprinted by kind
permission of Martin Secker and Warburg Limited,
London; and in the U.S.A. by kind permission of Alfred
A. Knopf, Inc., New York, copyright 1936 and renewed
1964 by Alfred A. Knopf, Inc.

YORK PRESS
Immeuble Esseily, Place Riad Solh, Beirut.

LONGMAN GROUP LIMITED
Burnt Mill,
Harlow, Essex

© Librairie du Liban 1982

First published 1982
ISBN 0 582 78261 9
Printed in Hong Kong by
Sing Cheong Printing Co Ltd

Contents

Part 1

Introduction

The life and times of Thomas Mann

Heinrich Mann considered his younger brother Thomas greater than himself. This is high praise, for Heinrich himself led an uncommonly fruitful life. He declined to stand for the Presidency of Germany. For several decades he was the leader of the European democrats. He exposed the shallow Imperial government of Germany, rightly predicting that it would take the country into a world war, and subsequently— long before most other observers—he warned of the dangers of the Nazi party. As a novelist he achieved unusual prominence. His early story *Im Schlaraffenland* (*Berlin: The Land of Cockaigne*, 1900), a satire of contemporary Germany, established him as the innovator of Expressionism.* His tragic tale of a teacher's love for a night-club singer, *Professor Unrat* (1905), was immortalised as the film *The Blue Angel*. From his voluminous works, an epic novel, *Henri IV* (1935), parodied the decadence of Germany between the wars, but offered in the symbolic figure of the loving, energetic, but misunderstood French King a humanitarian ideal that typified all Heinrich Mann's own actions and thoughts. For Thomas Mann to rank at least alongside his brother is, then, an extraordinary achievement. It is invidious to give precedence to either, for the dignity of their nation and the freedom of the German intellect depended very much on both.

Their father, Senator Mann, confronted by the poor school reports of his second son, cannot have dreamed of his subsequent success. The difficult little boy who hated school nevertheless went on to win the Nobel Prize for Literature, to see himself as the 'real Germany' when Adolf Hitler was burning first books and then cities, and to become the major German novelist of this century.

Thomas Mann was born on 6 June 1875 in Lübeck. His father, Thomas Johann Heinrich Mann, was a very shrewd businessman, who built up the family grain business, trading as far afield as Russia. He invested shrewdly in the new railways and steamboats, and became a widely respected Consul for the Royal Netherlands and then Senator

---

*A movement that embraced all the arts during the early years of the twentieth century. Through strident exclamations and bold, clashing colours it sought to expose an emotional state. Its very idealistic exponents looked to the 'New Man' to create better social conditions.

of the Hanseatic Free Town of Lübeck. His influence upon Thomas was lasting, and in *Lübeck als geistige Lebensform* (*Lübeck as a spiritual way of life*) Thomas recalled 'his dignity and common sense, his energy and industry, his personal and spiritual elegance, his social grace and humour, and the bonhomie with which he could talk to the common folk, who depended upon him in a genuinely filial way.' In other words, his father represented to Thomas what Consul Kröger is to Tonio, the epitome of the '*Bürgertum*', the educated, decent, practical, virtuous middle-class, the 'bourgeoisie' that embodied the finest qualities of the Germans. (The word has no hint of the sneer that sometimes greets its rather tawdry equivalent in France.) It is everything that young Hans Hansen will one day comfortably grace and perpetuate.

Yet Thomas Mann added thoughtfully: 'He was not a simple man, not strong, but nervous and sensitive.' This sensitivity was sharpened in Thomas by the characteristics that he inherited from his mother. Like Tonio's, Thomas's mother was an exotic lady, Julia da Silva-Bruhns, born in Brazil, the daughter of a plantation owner who himself originated from Lübeck, and of his Portuguese-Creole wife. Julia was, as Thomas Mann describes in *Lebensabriss* (*A Sketch of My Life*) 'distinctly Latin in type, in her youth a much-admired beauty and extraordinarily musical. When I ask myself the hereditary origin of my characteristics I am fain to recall Goethe's famous little verse and say that I too have from my father "*des Lebens ernstes Führen*" (the serious drive of life) but from my mother the "*Frohnatur*" (joyous nature)—the sensuous, artistic side, and in the widest sense, "*Lust zu fabulieren*" (the desire to create fables).'

The marriage was successful and she did not remarry when she moved to Munich after her husband's death. It is clear from this that some incidental details of Tonio's story are fictitious. In essence, though, both Thomas and Tonio inherited a mixture of tendencies and qualities that render the problems of both author and hero very similar.

The little boy grew up with his brothers, Heinrich and Karl Viktor, and his sisters, Julia and Carla, in a generally happy, literate household. Already he was drawn towards the enchantment of art, for he loved to listen to his mother, reading him Hans Andersen's fairy tales* in her foreign accent, and playing the haunting nocturnes and études of Chopin on the piano. Though he also loved his father, 'the wise representative of a century of middle-class diligence', Thomas already knew that he would never work for the family firm.

Tonio's school is clearly based on the Katharineum, the Lübeck grammar school that Thomas Mann detested. He needed five years to complete three grades, having to repeat two of them, and most of his

---

*Hans Christian Andersen (1805–75) was a renowned Danish story teller. Even as a child Thomas Mann was enchanted by the spirit of Denmark.

time there he spent in writing poetry. Theodor Storm was a distinguished former pupil of the school, and, not surprisingly, his plaintive verses spring to Tonio's lips whenever he is moved. Moreover, Tonio's friend Hans Hansen is also drawn from memory, for Thomas Mann's first works were his *Gedichte an einen Freund* (*Poems to a friend*), 'inscribed to a dear friend who as Hans Hansen in *Tonio Kröger* has a sort of symbolic existence, though in real life he took to drink and made a melancholy end in Africa'. The blue-eyed, fair-haired, confident Hans is modelled on Arnim Martens, and Thomas Mann wrote in 1955 in a letter to another school friend, Hermann Lange, from his home in Kilchberg, Switzerland, that 'him I *really* loved, and a more tender, blissful yet painful love I was never to experience for the rest of my life'.

Another revealing poem is his *Gedicht an eine Tanzstundenpartnerin* (*Poem to a dancing-class partner*) for here we see the prototype for Ingeborg Holm. With his sister Julia, Thomas attended dancing lessons in the winter of 1899. The affected Herr Knaak who so embarrasses Tonio derives from Rudolf Knoll, the Ballet Director of the German Theatre in Hamburg. In Mann's *A Sketch of my Life* he was to comment: 'What became of the flaxen-haired dancing partner who later was the object of love lyrics, I cannot say.' Thomas Mann's early set-backs in love are faithfully mirrored in Tonio's helpless passion for the cheerful, healthy Inge.

In 1891 Senator Mann died of blood poisoning. He was accorded an impressive funeral and was deeply mourned, for his liberal reforms had helped to prepare Lübeck for the twentieth century. The family grain business went into liquidation and now his widow decided to move to Munich. Spiritually she felt very much at home in Bavaria. An agricultural community, whose only important industry was brewing beer, Munich was the centre of artists, musicians and poets and was a merry, almost classless society. Like Frau Kröger, Frau Mann left the sterner climate of upper-middle-class Lübeck for the warmer, more relaxed world of the south.

Unlike Tonio, Thomas Mann did not lead a wild, libertine existence while he gradually matured as an author. Nevertheless, Munich and his holidays in Italy made him aware of a more liberated, sensual, sunny world than that of northern Germany. His zest for life was apparent in a host of enthusiasms. He loved to cycle; he acquired a dog, Titino; he went drinking with his fellow students; he listened enraptured to the music of the German composer Richard Wagner (1813–83); he read avidly the works of the German philosophers Friedrich Nietzsche (1844–1900) and Arthur Schopenhauer (1788–1860); and he travelled widely in Scandinavia and Italy. All these experiences would eventually impregnate his stories.

After an abortive stint as an apprentice at the South German Fire

Insurance Bank, Mann attended lectures as a student at the Technische Hochschule, preparing himself for a career in journalism, and eventually he became a copyreader for the satirical paper *Simplicissimus*. Moving now in literary circles he became the intimate friend of Kurt Martens (1870–1945)*, a novelist, to whom he soon dedicated *Tonio Kröger*. He moved to Marktstrasse 5, Schwabing, to an apartment on the fourth floor, and in such a place he sets the conversation between Lisabeta and Tonio.

In September 1899 a curious incident occurred when he returned to Lübeck on his way to Denmark and stayed at the Hotel Stadt Hamburg. Here he was all but arrested for fraud, and the irony of the situation amusingly and poignantly reappears in Tonio's misfortune. When Thomas Mann reached Aalsgaard and spent nine days in a hotel, he conceived the idea of his Novelle, *Tonio Kröger*.

Already he had written a few short stories and met with some success, but suddenly his reputation was assured. After three years of determined labour and many struggles with Fischer, his publisher, Thomas Mann at last saw the publication of *Buddenbrooks* in 1901, the novel which would one day win him the Nobel Prize for Literature. It deals with the devastating impact of an artistic temperament upon a solidly materialistic Lübeck family. When one reads *Tonio Kröger*, which focuses the problem upon one person, and turns back to *Buddenbrooks*, where the debilitating effect of art seeps through four generations, one seems almost to be looking at the same scene through different ends of a telescope.

Fame brought its inherent difficulties, though, for Thomas had offended both members of his family and the citizens of Lübeck, who easily recognised themselves and resented what they considered tasteless ingratitude. Years later the wounds healed at last, and Thomas Mann—by then an octogenarian—received the honorary citizenship of Lübeck from a town now proud to have occasioned so famous a novel.

He did not endear himself either to certain citizens of Munich, when he opted out of the Royal Bavarian Infantry Guards. He feigned an inflamed flat foot—an incident hilariously parodied in his comic novel *Felix Krull* (1954)—and when this failed, he used his mother's influence to free him from military service. His distaste for uniforms and martial glory anticipated the less selfish, more thoughtful and indeed heroic stand he was to take years later against those who revelled in nationalism and war.

With *Buddenbrooks* running into a fourth edition, Mann was now comfortably off. In 1902 he settled down at the home of his friend Dr von Hartungen, Villa Cristoforo in Riva on the Gardasee, and con-

*Martens wrote in Munich and Dresden. He took his own life after the air-raid on Dresden in 1945.

centrated on *Tonio Kröger*. In a letter to Kurt Martens he said: 'I am working just as usual, although very carefully and even more than usual line by line, because what I have in mind (a lengthy short story), is something so difficult that it will require considerable time.' (*Briefe I*).

Tonio Kröger was always to be Thomas Mann's own favourite work. Few stories have been so personal, not just in their background, but in the essential problem that dogged him even as he wrote. Moreover, a most conscientious stylist, he now sought to extend a technique he had already evolved in *Buddenbrooks*. He, who spent every spare moment at the Opera House, used the music he heard to mould his literary style. The whole question of the tormented artist faced by an uncomprehending society was itself raised to the level of music, the highest of the arts.

The story is elevated beyond even the immediate problem of the artist, and Tonio becomes the archetypal human being caught between two ways of life, unsure of his direction. Today, after two world wars and at a time when materialism is rampant, and social problems ever graver, Tonio remains as convincingly as ever a representative of mankind seeking to resolve the contradictions in life. The book was an instant success and in a letter to Carl Ehrenberg (*Briefe III*) Mann wrote: 'I have received 400 Marks. Please tell everyone about it!'

In a previous letter to him on 8 February 1903, Thomas Mann had jokingly signed himself 'Tonio Kröger', and in fact he might easily now have withdrawn into a world of art, remote from real life, had he not had the good fortune to meet Katja Pringsheim in the spring of 1903.

A beautiful girl of nineteen, she combined the charm of Ingeborg Holm with the intelligence and devotion of Magdalena Vermehren, and thus Tonio's perhaps artificial division of the world was reconciled. Now the artist could enjoy the fruits of 'real life' and yet pursue the higher calling of his spirit. Katja's father was Professor of Mathematics at Munich University and his wife a renowned beauty. Katja herself was the first girl in Bavaria to go to University, where she read mathematics under her father and physics under Röntgen. An extremely cultivated family, their salon, in Renaissance style hung with Gobelin tapestries, was the social and artistic centre of Munich. Thomas Mann fell in love at first sight, or second really, since later he discovered the charming coincidence that she was the little girl in the photograph he had cut out of a magazine and put over his desk as a schoolboy! To Heinrich he now wrote: 'Katja is a miracle, indescribably rare and precious, whose simple existence outweighs the cultural activities of fifteen writers or thirty painters!' After a frantic courtship, he eventually won her over and they were married in February 1905.

Throughout the vicissitudes of his public and private life she was a devoted wife, gave him four children, Klaus, Erika, Golo (now a distinguished historian) and Monika, and was a loyal comforter of her brother-in-law Heinrich during his impoverished exile in California. It is a happy irony that the master ironist himself, at the moment when he revealed Tonio's agonised feelings, was basking in blissful love of Katja. He wrote of their meeting: 'Up to then, where I had loved I had always at the same time despised. The mingling of longing and contempt, ironic love, had been my most characteristic emotion. Tonio Kröger loved "life", blue-eyed commonness, nostalgically, mockingly and hopelessly. And now? A being sweet as the world, and also good and also uncommon, and also able (though perhaps not willing) to meet me with intelligence and kindness: something absolutely and incredibly new! This love, the strongest there can be, is from this point of view—whatever may happen—my first and only *happy* love.'

The novel *Königliche Hoheit* (*Royal Highness*, 1909) was a tribute to his wife and an antidote to *Tonio Kröger*. Mann needed the security of his marriage, for severe shocks were imminent. His sister Carla, an actress who had failed to find her way in the exotic, theatrical life that Tonio calls the 'gypsy' world, committed suicide at their mother's home. Much later his other sister 'Lula' and then his own son Klaus were to take their own lives. To someone with so profound a sense of the family bonds, these were terrible blows. Dreadful too was the rift with his closest friend, his brother Heinrich, and it was the Great War of 1914-18 that brought their quarrel to a head.

As Europe edged precariously towards the War, Thomas Mann was writing *Der Tod in Venedig* (*Death in Venice*, 1913). In this famous short story the artist—the author Gustav von Aschenbach—is lured to destruction by the fatal attraction of beauty, embodied in the lovely child, Tadzio. Mann had now taken Tonio's problem to its logical conclusion. Either Tonio must die, like Aschenbach, or he must come down into the real world, like Hans Castorp, the hero of *Der Zauberberg* (*The Magic Mountain*, 1924), adapting the elevated mountain-tops of art and philosophy to the problems of everyday life. It required a world war to bring not just Hans Castorp, but Thomas Mann himself, down into the world again. Indeed, he was only a third of the way through *The Magic Mountain* when the First World War broke out in August 1914. Heinrich was appalled to see his brother quietly enjoying the bourgeois comforts of his new home in Poschingerstrasse and ignoring the cruel realities of the War as he continued his novel. Indeed Thomas defended the German role in the War, praising its cleansing powers and recalling the heroic efforts of Frederick the Great to create the German nation. The very title of his work *Betrachtungen eines Unpolitischen* (*Reflections of a Non-political Man*, 1918) emphasised his distaste for his brother's passionate involvement.

For years now Heinrich, from his home in democratic France, had urged a less authoritarian, less militaristic government for Imperial

Germany. His epic novel *Der Untertan* (*The Man of Straw*, 1918) violently and tragically depicted its core and effectively summarised his contempt for the dictatorial splendour of the nationalistic German Empire. He appealed yet again for democracy before it was too late. He foresaw all too clearly (and unfashionably) the suffering that must ensue. For three years the brothers communicated only by letter, and it is very moving to witness Heinrich's loving, loyal efforts to bring Thomas to recognise the facts: 'The hour will come, I hope, when you will see people, not shadows, and then perhaps—me.'

Years later Thomas Mann acknowledged that his own progression from self-indulgent nationalism to a more objective and mature view of politics was also the 'problem of the German nation'. Gradually he came to see the sanity of Heinrich's point of view. Their reconciliation was cemented when Heinrich fell dangerously ill and Thomas rushed to his bedside. Fairly enough, Thomas Mann explained that although his views might have been modified, his essential goal was unchanged: he sought the well-being of German humanity.

Still writing extensively, he watched the birth of the Weimar Republic (1919–33) and now shoulder to shoulder with Heinrich rebuked the failure of the Germans to acknowledge their guilt and even defeat in the War. The brothers could see how the precarious financial situation, not just of Germany but of the world, endangered the peace of Europe. They witnessed the swirling tides of nationalism and anti-semitism, and warned against a dictatorship.

Meanwhile Thomas Mann celebrated his fiftieth birthday, at the Old Council Hall in Munich, replying to countless tributes in words that would contrast tellingly with the meriticious nonsense of the Nazis: 'It is a wonderful, gratifying thing to belong to a great cultural people like the Germans, to use their language, to be permitted to follow and continue to develop their great heritage' (*Tischrede bei der Feier des fünfzigsten Geburtstages*) (*Speech at the Fiftieth Birthday Celebrations*, 1925). Profoundly conscious that he and his brother were carrying on the traditions of Goethe* and Schiller,† he accepted the Nobel Prize for Literature in 1929, seeing it as a mark of world sympathy for his 'wounded and misunderstood people'.

When the German economy collapsed and the rise of Hitler grew ever more certain, Thomas Mann launched his *Appeal to Reason* in 1930;

*Johann Wolfgang von Goethe (1749–1832), greatest of German writers, achieved prominence as a scientist and political leader in Weimar. His lyric poetry and his epic *Faust* (Part 1, 1818: Part 2, 1832) stand out among his diverse works. To Thomas Mann, who celebrated his genius in *Lotte in Weimar* (1939), Goethe symbolised the peak of German cultural life.
†Johann Christoph Friedrich Schiller (1759–1805), a major German playwright whose masterpieces range from the turbulent *Die Räuber* (*The Robbers*, 1780) to the classical tragedies of his later years, such as the trilogy *Wallenstein* (1799) and *Maria Stuart* (1800).

and his friend, the conductor Bruno Walter, had to help him escape from Nazi hecklers in the Beethovensaal in Berlin. In need of a holiday, he went to Egypt to acquire material for his massive four-volume novel *Joseph und Seine Brüder* (*Joseph and his Brothers*, 1933-43). The work would take a decade to accomplish, and in retelling the biblical story the author again showed his love of humanity. The very title of the last volume, *Joseph the Provider*, is a blow against such men as Hitler, for it emphasises the interdependence of human beings.

The character of Joseph owed much to President Roosevelt,* who received Thomas Mann at the White House in 1935. By now Mann was, with his brother, the voice of civilised Germany, and both were advocating a spirit of European Social Democracy. The mutual admiration of Roosevelt and Thomas Mann is entirely appropriate, for by the gun and the pen they were allies against Hitler, who on 19 August 1934 had been confirmed as absolute dictator of Germany by some 38 million votes out of 43 million.

Between his warnings against nationalism and his work on *Joseph*, Mann found time to write *Lotte in Weimar* (1939). In recapturing the genius of Goethe, Mann again held up to the Germans a courageous reminder of all that they were destroying—literally destroying, moreover, for by now Heinrich Mann's works were publicly burned. Another three years of agonising now attended Thomas. If he spoke out against the Nazis his own books would be burned, and he felt he could best serve the nation by publishing their humanitarian message. Accused of time-serving and treason by those who misunderstood his silence, he finally spoke in the most dramatic way possible. He proposed that Carl von Ossietzky (1889-1938), former editor of *Weltbühne* (*World Stage*) and now imprisoned in a Nazi concentration camp, a martyr to the principle of peace, be given the Nobel Peace Prize. To Hitler's fury, the Prize was awarded.

The German government immediately charged Mann with 'treasonable attacks on the Reich'. He was swift to emulate his brother's example and accepted the offer of Czechoslovakian citizenship on 19 November 1936. Bonn University withdrew his honorary doctorate and Mann replied with a dignified analysis of the Nazi movement. National Socialism, he said, was depriving the people of their freedoms for the unique purpose of all-out war. Without a war, the very existence of the Nazi Party would be pointless. Thus in a few words he indicated the anarchical futility of the movement.

Now Thomas Mann had declared open war on Hitler. With biting irony he called him his 'Brother', seeing the Führer and himself as the two contrasting expressions of the German soul. While his fame grew

*Franklin Delano Roosevelt (1882-1945), thirty-second President (1933-45) of the United States of America.

and Yale University opened the Thomas Mann Library to contain his archives, which he described as his efforts to extract form from chaos, the world itself was tumbling into a nightmare. In May 1939 Thomas Mann and Albert Einstein* received honorary doctorates from Princeton. They, who embodied the highest expression of the German intellect in this century, were to see—four months later—the fulfilment of the lowest inclinations of the German nation, for Hitler invaded Poland and the Second World War had begun.

Thomas Mann had made four lecture tours to the United States of America, and he decided to settle there for the duration of the War. In October 1940 he began to make monthly broadcasts, *Deutsche Hörer!* (*German Listeners!*) via the British Broadcasting Corporation to the people of Germany, saying: 'In war-time there is no way left for the written word to pierce the wall which the tyrants have erected round you.' Ceaselessly writing against the Nazis, he accepted the post of Consultant in Germanic literature of the library of Congress, and finally in January 1944 he and Katja became American citizens.

On 6 June 1944 Mann wrote: 'I could not help but see a meaningful dispensation, one of the harmonies of my life, in the fact that the longed for, the scarcely-thought possible event, was taking place on this day, my day' (*The Genesis of a Novel*, 1961). It was D-Day. The British and American troops had landed in Normandy on Mann's sixty-ninth birthday. With renewed hope, he continued his latest novel, *Dr Faustus* (1947). The theme was best known in Germany through Goethe's masterpiece. Now Thomas Mann reworked the legend, and through the tragic, lonely life of the musical genius Adrian Leverkühn he reflected the fate of Germany. Already he had often marvelled at the 'intoxicating self-annihilation' of Wagner's music. Hanno Buddenbrook, Tonio Kröger, Gustav von Aschenbach had all sensed the devastating power of artistic genius. Now the evil genius of Germany, sublimated in Hitler's demonic urge towards his own catastrophic Twilight of the Gods, showed Mann, himself very sick with lung cancer, the fearful outcome of unrestrained Dionysiac frenzy. The Devil promises Adrian 'sacred ecstasy', and symbolically Germany sells its soul. Only through the dreadful conflagration of world war can she be cleansed and rise again. As in the First World War, Mann saw warfare as an agent of purification, but this time it had become not something proudly inflicted on others, but a terrifying punishment.

By the time *Dr Faustus* was completed in January 1947, the War had been over for more than a year. Though his cancer was successfully

*Albert Einstein (1879-1955), a theoretical physicist who formulated the Theory of Relativity. Acknowledged in his own lifetime as one of the great thinkers of mankind, he had to flee Nazi oppression because of his Jewish ancestry, leaving Germany for America in 1933.

checked, problems beset Thomas Mann. In the USA an atmosphere of suspicion made life intolerable for many artists accused (usually wrongly) of communist tendencies, and American democracy seemed to be lurching into some form of authoritarianism. Denying that he had ever been a communist, he still felt that 'this insanity and persecution mania' would lead to even worse consequences than communism itself ('*Ich stelle fest*', *Aufbau*, New York, 13 April 1951). In Germany, Mann was accused of cowardice by those writers who had remained in Europe during the War. His decision not to return yet awhile to Germany, a country 'that has become alien to me', also caused much criticism. He returned in fact in 1949, for the first time in sixteen years. Though now an American citizen, his conscience was clear, for he had never abandoned his cultural home, the German language. The Goethe Prize of the city of Frankfurt and the honorary citizenship of Weimar were the climax of a vivid, painful, but valuable visit.

The deaths of his brothers and his son Klaus overshadowed all else in 1950, and he sought relief in the joyous humour of a novel he had begun forty years before, *Felix Krull* (1954). He interrupted this novel yet again to write *Die Betrogene* (*The Black Swan*, 1953), a bitter novel of disillusionment that suggests the despair so near to overwhelming him. Soon, though, he reverted to the gaiety of his tale of a confidence trickster. His last novel evoked universal enthusiasm and heart-felt mirth, qualities that Mann placed artistically higher than the smile raised by irony.

His own life ended on a similarly heartening note. His last major work was a tribute to the great German idealist, Friedrich Schiller, and the culmination of Mann's life was perhaps the honorary citizenship which Lübeck conferred on him on 20 May 1955. Next day he read from *Tonio Kröger* in the Lübeck Stadttheater, and this time the real Tonio was received not as a criminal on the run but as the town's most distinguished son. Already on 6 May 1955 he had broadcast the entire story over Northwest German Radio from sunset to midnight, and it had been very well received. His eightieth birthday brought tributes from all over the world. On 12 August calcification of a leg artery caused his death in the Zurich Canton Hospital, and he was buried in the cemetery at Kilchberg. In the words of the French author François Mauriac (1885–1970): 'In time of subjection he was able to remain a liberal spirit. He has preserved the honour of Germany.'

The literary background

Tonio Kröger is a Novelle. This German word denotes a 'novella', an extended short story. It is a popular *genre* in German Literature. It concentrates upon one essential idea, and unlike the novel—which can delve at leisure into the incidental details of the plot and the characterisation—it restricts itself severely to one event or conflict that will alter the lives of all those involved. *Buddenbrooks* and *Tonio Kröger* clearly demonstrate this fundamental distinction.

Often a central symbol exemplifies the problem. In *Die Schwarze Spinne* (1842) by Jeremias Gotthelf (1797-1854), for instance, the black spider of the title represents the devilish side of man's nature, which he must learn to subdue. In *Romeo und Julia auf dem Dorfe* (1874), by Gottfried Keller (1819-90), the village Romeo and Juliet are destroyed by the conflict between their fathers, a tragedy vividly symbolised by the wall of stones they build between their fields. There is usually a *Wendepunkt*, a turning-point, in these stories: it is that moment when someone takes an irreversible step and thereafter his fate is decided. When, for example, the fathers in Keller's story decide to steal a strip of land from a field they do not own, the sin inevitably leads to hatred, despair and the suicide of the innocent children.

The stories are usually told with extreme detachment. In this way the author can analyse deeply personal conflicts and moments of passionately subjective lyricism in a cool, objective manner. This raises the story to a symbolical level, and what to the characters is their own intimate tragedy becomes for the reader a comment upon life of universal application. The Novelle by Theodor Storm that so moves Tonio, for instance, transports us beyond the localised story to the broader theme of lost childhood.

The central symbol of the Novelle *Tonio Kröger* is plainly stated in the title. Tonio's first name comes to represent art, the warm south, his mother's influence, the bohemian world and the creative stirrings in his soul. His surname stands for life, the cold north, his father's influence, the respectable bourgeois world, and his yearning to belong to a normal uncomplicated society.

The turning point of the Novelle is carefully prepared and thoroughly plausible. After the scenes from Tonio's youth, which paint for us the conflict within him, he is faced with a choice. Symbolically he elects to leave Munich and return to the north, and thus clearly states his love of life. As Professor Wilkinson says, 'in the inner world of the Spirit it is a moment of rebirth'.* The very form of the Novelle alters at this crucial moment. Until now it has been, in Mann's own words, a 'ballad in prose', each 'verse' relating a different episode of Tonio's life. Now the long monologues slow the story down, and Tonio himself stands back to reflect upon his life and so to decide upon his future. Then the ballad continues its musical way, tracing Tonio's subsequent life, with its haunting echoes of his youth. Now, however, he relives his earlier experiences with the wisdom of one who is no longer a confused, un-

*In *Tonio Kröger*, Blackwell, Oxford, 1968, p.xxxv.

happy child, but a man who has openly admitted where his deepest feelings lie.

Tonio Kröger is the quintessential Novelle, for its very theme is lyricism. The crux of the tale is the conflict in Tonio between his love of art and his love of life, a struggle at once exhilarating and desperate, to which he eventually learns to reconcile himself. Mann's own objective, ironic picture of his fictitious self gives shape to Tonio's life, just as Tonio hopes to give shape to the life around him, and thus the envious, longing, but blissful Tonio is raised to the symbolic status of a man seeking to draw together the conflicting elements within his soul.

A note on the text

Tonio is the author's spiritual twin. Not surprisingly, therefore, Mann first described the young writer in verse. The lyrical tone of the Novelle, its musical refrains, and its very theme make it almost a poem about a poet. At the very end of 1900 Thomas had already hinted to Heinrich that he intended to write an 'elegiac short story', and soon afterwards he had chosen a revealing provisional title, *Literatur*. Excitedly he turned from the ineluctable decline of the Buddenbrook family, healthy Lübeck merchants rendered impotent by the deathly charms of art, towards the more hopeful tale of *Tonio Kröger*. He told Heinrich that not everything in him had been 'distorted, corroded, laid waste by cursed literature'. Anticipating Tonio's lament that the writer must 'die to life', he added that 'literature is death': 'I shall never understand how one can be enslaved by it without hating it bitterly.' Tonio avoids such hatred, for his love of everyday life gives purpose to his art, which in return gives shape and meaning to life.

Mann wrote the story with the care of an artist painting a miniature. His personal satisfaction was life-long, and the public's appreciation instantaneous. In 1903 it was published along with *Tristan*. This in itself reflected Mann's renewed faith in life, for *Tristan* mercilessly mocks the Wagnerian death wish of Herr Spinell, who symbolically runs away from a pram at the end of the book; he cannot match the healthy challenge of real life expressed in 'the youthful Klötjahn's joyous screams'.

Tonio Kröger ends in an altogether happier frame of mind with 'no little innocent bliss'. Ever since its first appearance, the reading public has recognised in Tonio a mirror of its own confusions and found solace in his conclusions. Mrs H.T. Lowe-Porter's excellent translation brought the story before the English-speaking world in conjunction with *Tristan* and *Death in Venice*, published by Secker & Warburg, London, 1928. Some of *Tonio Kröger*'s enduring fame must stem from its companion piece. *Death in Venice* brilliantly evokes the decay of the writer von Aschenbach in the plague ridden, sinking city of Venice. The lovely summoner Tadzio hypnotises the artist and dooms him. The story beautifully but tragically leads to the end of one road that faces Tonio. Later works explore different and more hopeful paths, but the persuasive power of *Death in Venice*, and the discussion provoked by Luchino Visconti's film of the same name, helped to attract readers almost incidentally to *Tonio Kröger*. The award of the 1929 Nobel Prize had guaranteed a renewed interest in Mann's early works. Half a century more has confirmed their universal appeal.

Quotations from the text are taken from *Death in Venice*; *Tristan*; *Tonio Kröger* (translated by H.T. Lowe-Porter, 1928), Penguin Modern Classics, Penguin Books, Harmondsworth, 1971; 1977 reprint. This translation is available in the U.S.A. in Thomas Mann, *Stories of Three Decades*, Alfred A. Knopf, New York, 1936.

Part 2

Summaries
of TONIO KRÖGER

A general summary

Tonio Kröger's personality derives from the strict morality of his northern father and the freer, exotic, Mediterranean tendencies of his mother. He is at home neither in the world of the bourgeois nor of the gypsy, and the conflicts in his character affect his relationships throughout the story. As a child he is a romantic dreamer who yearns for the friendship of the fair-haired, blue-eyed, conventional and happy Hans. Later the blonde, blue-eyed Ingeborg is indifferent to his love, for he appeals only to those as soulful as himself.

In time the sensual experiences of the south are worked into fine literature by his icy intellect, but as he confesses to his friend Lisabeta, he feels an outcast, a criminal even, yearning for the love of ordinary people. To create, he laments, he must 'die to life'. Lisabeta sees him as a failed bourgeois.

Denmark offers the prospect of a healthy change. On his way he returns to his home town and finds his family house has become the Public Library. He is even taken for an escaped criminal, yet somehow feels this is only right and proper. At sea and on the Danish beaches he finds exhilaration in nature and, sometimes, peace of mind, until one day at a hotel dance two people identical in appearance to Hans and Inge revive his yearnings, and again he feels cruelly cut off from the banal dance of life. Even so he is happy in his way, for as an artist he will give form and meaning to the commonplace life he envies, longs for, despises somewhat, but above all, loves.

Detailed summaries

Part 1

On a wet, windy day the children stream out of school. One of them, the fourteen-year-old Tonio, is waiting for his friend, Hans Hansen, for they have arranged to walk home together. Hans, however, has clearly forgotten all about it and Tonio is deeply hurt. Seeing this, Hans invents an excuse about the weather and to Tonio's delight agrees again to the walk.

Tonio feels different from the other children, whose happy confidence is epitomised in Hans, a handsome, practical, fair-haired, blue-eyed boy, liked and admired by all. Tonio, on the other hand, has the dark complexion and dreamy looks of Consuelo, his Mediterranean mother. An introspective child, he analyses his sufferings almost with pleasure. He lives in a world of poetry to the sounds of his violin, the fountain by the walnut tree, and the North Sea.

Nevertheless, he yearns for the friendship of the uncomplicated Hans, who lives in harmony with all the world. From his father, Consul Kröger, Tonio has inherited a sense of what is dignified and respectable: 'after all, we are not gypsies living in a green wagon', and thus he envies Hans his easy confidence. He does not seek to emulate him, merely to win his friendship. Even so, he hopes against hope to arouse in Hans some of his own poetic awareness.

He tells Hans about the play he has just read, Schiller's *Don Carlos*, in which the King, thinking himself betrayed by his one friend, weeps for loneliness. Hans, more interested in his books on horses, but anxious not to hurt Tonio, asks about the betrayal. Just then another boy, Irwin Immerthal, greets Hans. They discuss riding lessons, and, to Tonio's chagrin, Hans now calls him 'Kröger'. Almost in tears, Tonio agrees that his is a silly, foreign name.

Later, Hans remorsefully promises to read *Don Carlos*. Overjoyed, Tonio walks back up the wet, windy street. He hopes Hans will never change. 'His heart beat richly: longing was awake in it, and a gentle envy; a faint contempt, and no little innocent bliss.'

NOTES AND GLOSSARY:

school: in 1899 Thomas Mann was sent to the Katharineum School in Lübeck: 'School I loathed . . . I was critical of the manners of its despots, and soon found myself in a sort of literary opposition to its spirit, its discipline and its methods of teaching.'* Like Tonio, he was unpopular, for he wrote verse which he showed to the others 'out of vanity'

Olympian . . . master: in Mann's last public speech, a tribute to Schiller on the 150th anniversary of the poet's death, he recalled with respect his teacher, Dr Baethcke, who had impressed upon him the greatness of Schiller. Tonio's teacher is probably based upon Dr Baethcke. As an intellectual, he appears to the inchoate artist, Tonio, to have the attributes of a god: Mount Olympus was the home of the Greek gods; Jupiter was King of the Roman gods; Wotan

*Lebensabriss (trans. H. Lowe-Porter), Secker and Warburg, London, 1931.

or Woden was the son of Thor, and Allfather of the Scandinavian gods: he was also god of the dead and of cunning, poetry and wisdom, all of which lend themselves nicely to Tonio's theory that the artist must 'die to life'

Tonio Kröger: as Tonio explains himself, his name is short for Antonio, a typically Mediterranean name that symbolises—quite consciously in his case—his sensual, artistic leanings. Kröger, with its harsher, gutteral sounds, emphasises the prosaic qualities that he inherits from his German father. The names therefore have a discordant ring in Hans's ears

Consul Kröger: the Free City of Lübeck was controlled by the Senate and the Citizens' Council. The twenty Senators, elected for life, exercised much power, and were assisted by the 120 Councillors of the 'Bürgerschaft', who were elected by the various guilds and professional bodies. Thomas Mann's grandfather, Johann Sigmund, was a Consul whose fortune was built (like Tonio's father's) upon grain. Mann's father expanded the business, became Councillor for the Marienkirche district of Lübeck in 1869, and rose to the rank of Senator in 1877

old ancestral home: immortalised in *Buddenbrooks*, Thomas Mann's home in Lübeck's Mengstrasse is in essence that of Tonio's in his unnamed home-town

gypsies: the gypsies are a wandering race of Hindu origin, called by themselves Romany: with their dark complexions, mysterious customs and nomadic habits, passing through the country to peddle their wares and read fortunes in their brightly coloured wagons, they symbolise for Tonio his restless, exotic, and even suspect qualities

Schiller's *Don Carlos*: Friedrich Schiller (1759-1805) epitomised for Thomas Mann the type of writer, like his own brother Heinrich Mann, who reminds men of the moral courage of which they are capable. Schiller's *Don Carlos* (1787) is a tragedy based on the Principe de Asturias (1545-68), who was arrested by his father, Philip II of Spain, as a danger to the State, and died in prison

Part 2

At sixteen, no longer a 'little, stupid boy', Tonio sees Ingeborg Holm at a dancing class in Frau Hustede's drawing-room. He falls in love with the girl with the thick blonde plait, laughing blue eyes and freckled face. Aware that love will bring him pain, he is still glad, for it will also make him rich and vital, a state he prefers to one of tranquil order.

Such calm confidence is exemplified by Herr Knaak, the dancing master. Tonio sees the essential stupidity beneath his overpowering pride and elastic elegance. Knaak's beautiful brown eyes will never see the melancholy complexities of life, and that makes him lovable. No wonder the simple, blonde Inge admires him.

Tonio yearns for Inge's love, yet she is indifferent to him. He panics when he finds himself in her set in a quadrille, and painfully recalls a line from Storm's poem: 'I would sleep, but thou must dance.' In his confusion he ends up among the girls, and is saddened that Inge laughs at him with the others.

Tonio himself is indifferent to the adoration of Magdalena Vermehren, a clumsy, serious, poetic girl who appreciates his verses. It hurts him to think that when he is famous she will be impressed, but blue-eyed Inge will not care.

Standing in front of a blind, gazing into himself, 'the theatre of so much pain and longing', he wonders why he is not reading *Immensee* in his room and listening to the moaning of the old walnut tree in the twilight. Yet he feels that his place *is* here near Inge, near the noise and laughter, even if he must be aloof and lonely.

Even so he is happy, for happiness lies not in being loved, but in loving. He vows to be faithful at the altar of love, but despite his efforts the flame quietly dies out, for Tonio has his own ambitions to fulfil.

NOTES AND GLOSSARY:

Ingeborg Holm: Inge's name is as uncompromisingly North European as Hans Hansen's, and it suits her simple nature. She recalls Mann's real dancing partner when he was a boy. Moreover, in Florence in May 1901, Thomas Mann had fallen in love with a very pretty blonde English girl with the equally simple name of Mary Smith, and the physical details of Mary and Inge have much in common. However, Thomas Mann felt Mary to be too clever for him and marriage plans were quietly dropped. Significantly, he was also worried that their difference in nationality might affect their marriage—a hint at the confusion that Tonio has inherited

François Knaak:	the elegant French Christian name jars against the harsh Germanic surname, and helps to suggest the basic fraudulence of this exquisite dancing master; a Hamburger, he has presumably changed his first name for effect. The name anticipates that of Mann's hilarious confidence trickster, Felix Krull. In much the same way, Max Beerbohm suggests the hard-boiled businesswoman beneath an exotic appearance by calling his comic heroine Zuleika Dobson
Knaak's French:	in introducing himself he should say: '*J'ai l'honneur de me présenter . . . Je m'appelle Knaak.*' His impossible grammar underlines his superficiality, for his next words are intended to suggest that his French is perfect
the dances:	the ladies observe the dances through *lorgnettes*— eye-glasses held on a handle. Knaak first teaches the *mazurka*—a lively Polish dance like the polka, in triple time. Then comes the *quadrille*—a square dance for four couples, containing five figures; this requires careful attention, for the dancers have to follow a strict pattern. The French dancing terms again enable Knaak to show off. *En avant* is the order to advance. *Compliment* is the bow to one's partner. *Moulinet des dames, tour de main* bids the ladies join hands and twirl in a circle. Tonio, lost in his unhappy dreams, forgets that he must wait for the girls to finish their turn and ends up among them. *En arrière* bids him to return to the boys. *Fi donc* is an expression of mock horror
Storm:	(Hans) Theodor Woldsen (1817–88). Mann was strongly influenced by the tender, world-weary realism of this North German poet's *Liederbuch dreier Freunde* (1843) and *Gedichte* (1852). Tonio is thinking of his poem *Hyazinthen*, the title of which evokes both the beauty of the hyacinth and the youth whom Apollo loved. Tonio, hurt by unrequited love, quotes from the first verse. Lost in darkness, amidst the fragrant flowers, thinking only of his beloved, the poet seeks sleep—a symbol of oblivion, free from the cares of life, love and art. The loved ones, though, 'must dance'. For Storm and for Tonio the dance symbolises the bustle of happiness and life

Immensee: in his *Betrachtungen eines Unpolitischen* Thomas Mann describes *Tonio Kröger* as an updated version of Storm's short story, *Immensee* (1852), which tells of the vanished happiness of childhood. It is not surprising that in his melancholy mood Tonio should identify with the book, even while he is still very young

Part 3

He goes his way, and if he goes wrong it is because 'for some people there is no right way'. With the death of his father and the remarriage of his mother, the house is sold and the business dissolved, and Tonio begins to lose touch with his early life, even to look down on it. Standing apart from normal, cheerful life, he sees its comedy and tragedy. His own life in the south is a mixture of lust and yearning for purity; despising his existence, he is flung between the extremes of an icy intellect and his scorching senses. As his health suffers, his style grows ever more refined. He sees that to create his art, he must cease to exist as a human being.

NOTES AND GLOSSARY:

the decline of the family: the family '*war nach und nach in einen Zustand des Abbröckelns und der Zersetzung geraten*': this 'gradual decline from the material to the artistic worlds' is the theme and indeed sub-title of *Buddenbrooks*

Part 4

In Munich he calls on Lisabeta Ivanovna, a painter who, like himself, is just over thirty years old and has dark features. The confused lines on her canvas remind him of his own confused thoughts. The smell of paint and fixative contrast with the fragrance of the spring, and this too reflects the conflict in his own mind: the fixative recalls the creation of his literary art, whilst he quails before the naturalness and triumphant youth of the spring.

He cannot emulate his friend Adalbert, a novelist, who escapes from the real world of the spring into the neutral, rarified atmosphere of a café, for Tonio requires real life around him, against which to react. He continues to wear elegant clothes, for his thoughts are bohemian enough already. He feels like a 'castrato', producing beautiful art at the cost of his personal humanity: for as a writer he must stand aloof from the warm, heartfelt, but essentially futile life around him. Yet he admits that he is growing sick to death of the artist's obligations, of the remoteness that is the requisite of good taste.

He recalls a great actor who suffered in the same way: off-stage he was morbidly self-conscious and unstable. Similarly a prince in disguise will still be conscious that he is something odd, different, inimical.

Average, comfortable human beings see in a great artist a 'gift'. They do not realise that this 'gift' is in fact a sinister, almost criminal, affair. He recalls a banker, whose stories stemmed not from his experiences in prison but from the qualities that put him in prison in the first place. Wagner's *Tristan and Isolde* (1859) will arouse enthusiasm in the normal, healthy man, whereas the true artist will find in it something morbid and profoundly equivocal.

Lisabeta points out that the artist can be considered as a saint, redeeming the world through the understanding, forgiveness and love invoked by the power of literature. Tonio admits that Russian writers nearly achieve this.

He returns to the question of the artist's 'knowledge'. An artist observes the world with all its sadness and even torture and yet must remain cheerfully objective, 'in the sublime consciousness of moral superiority over the horrible invention of existence'. Yet sometimes the writer finds it simply indecent and outrageous to remain aloof and smiling. His gaze is 'blinded with feeling'. Hamlet, 'that typical literary man', suffered in this way. Often, too, the writer, whilst ironically expounding the truth, is mocked by society as naive and stupid.

Tonio rejects the idea of the redeeming power of literature, for it is nihilistic: by 'putting feelings on ice', analysing and labelling them as though they are finished for ever, the writer thinks he has redeemed the world, but in fact the world goes on acting and sinning. And Tonio is glad of this, for he loves life. By 'life' he does not mean the wild, extraordinary, daemonic, ruthless philosophy of a Caesar Borgia, eternally opposed to the artistic, intellectual way of life. He means the banal, innocent bliss of the commonplace. He yearns for simple human friendship.

Until now his friends and admirers have always been the poor and the suffering, who see poetry as a mild revenge on real life, 'people who are always falling down in the dance'. He yearns for the unthinking blue-eyed ones. And they should remain like this, with their books on horses—it is wrong to try to win them over to the sickly, melancholy world of poetry.

What is more pitiable than 'life led astray by art'? Tonio recalls a lieutenant he admired, until he embarrassed a happy, healthy party by reading his verses. He should have known that you cannot 'pluck a single leaf from the laurel tree of art without paying for it with your life'.

Lisabeta tells the crestfallen Tonio that he is 'a bourgeois on the wrong path, a bourgeois manqué'.
Resolutely he goes home, glad to have expressed his views.

NOTES AND GLOSSARY:

the literary discussion: Mann wrote in *Die neue Rundschau* (1930) of this passage that 'lyric and prose essay in one, the conversation with the entirely imaginary Russian friend cost me months'

Lisabeta Ivanovna: the artist's Russian name, her Russian cigarettes (*papyros*) and her friendly name of 'little father' ('Batuschka') for Tonio, all emphasise the remoteness of her world from that of the respectable merchant, Consul Kröger. Her age, just over thirty, is about the same as Tonio's, whereas Thomas Mann was twenty-seven at the time of writing in 1903

Munich: after the death of Senator Mann, his widow took Thomas and the other children in 1894 to an apartment in the north of Munich, in Schwabing, close to Schellingstrasse where Lisabeta works. A cheerful university town in Bavaria, it was famous for its music, its beer, and its coffee-houses, and was the Montmartre of the German painters and poets. 'My mother loved the south, the mountains, Munich . . .', wrote Thomas Mann in *A Sketch of my Life*, and a link with Tonio's mother is apparent

bohemian: Tonio does not want to dress in the conventionally untidy style of an 'artist', for that would be to descend to Knaak's level of showmanship. As he says, his mind is gypsy-like enough already. Thomas Mann himself was 'courteous, well-dressed, discrete, and pleasantly bourgeois' in appearance, to use his own description of his friend Kurt Martens, to whom he dedicated *Tonio Kröger*. As his wife jokingly observed, he was usually taken for a commercial traveller

unsexed papal singers: image drawn from the 'castrati' of the Vatican choirs, whose beautiful singing was achieved only at the inhuman cost of castration

Tristan and Isolde: Richard Wagner (1813–83) wrote the opera in 1865. Its influence on Mann was considerable. The irresistible lure of death to the passionate lovers is, for Thomas Mann, the ultimate example of the wild, shapeless, Dionysiac forces in man which will destroy him unless he opposes them with all the might of morality, form and conscience. His own short story *Tristan* grotesquely parodies the dangerous effect of unrestrained art upon life, for Wagner's music kills the consumptive heroine. Similarly little Hanno in *Buddenbrooks* is a prey to the fatal seductiveness of the music, and his death brings the merchant family to an untimely end

Horatio: in Shakespeare's *Hamlet* (1603), Horatio, the young Prince of Denmark's friend, is a practical man, who points out the dangers of considering a matter 'too curiously', for if one studies a problem too closely its very profundity and complexity will paralyse the will to solve it. Hans Hansen has much in common with Horatio, but Hamlet cannot be content with a superficial view, however sensible it may be: 'There are more things in heaven and earth, Horatio,/ Than are dreamt of in your philosophy' (*Hamlet* I, 5, 166)

Hamlet: the intellectual Prince learns from his father's ghost that his uncle Claudius has murdered his father in order to seize the throne and marry Hamlet's mother. Sickened by his knowledge, Hamlet wonders if any action is really worthwhile. By thinking so much, he loses the urge to act. This is precisely the danger contained in the French novel *Corinne* (1807) by Madame de Stael (1766–1817), which Tonio quotes: '*Tout comprendre c'est tout pardonner*'—to understand everything is to forgive everything. Tonio feels very close to Hamlet, for as an intellectual himself he reduces life to the mere written word, and what was warm and real can thus become as empty and pointless as revenge and life itself sometimes seem to Hamlet

Caesar Borgia: Borgia (1476–1507) was the son of Pope Alexander VI. His family rose to power at the Vatican by murdering their enemies, usually with poison. Caesar, whose family motto was *Aut Caesar aut nihil* (either Caesar or nothing), here symbolises the wild, Dionysiac forces extolled by Nietzsche* and

*Friedrich Nietzsche (1844–1900), a profoundly influential German philosopher, who saw in mankind an urge to dominate, which he called the 'Will to Power', and who sought to channel these wilder instincts into a fruitful self-control, which would serve the community.

Wagner. These may create masterpieces of art, but they can also inspire great evil, as Hitler was to prove. Tonio's moral rejection of such 'savage greatness' stems from his 'bourgeois' father and foreshadows Mann's own political and artistic attitudes later in his life

Part 5

Tonio tells Lisabeta that he is taking a holiday. He rejects the sensual, soulless, black-eyed Italians, preferring Denmark with its healthy literature and food, and prosaic names like Ingeborg. He wants to stand where the noble souled Hamlet found despair and death at Kronberg. Blushing, he admits that he will call in at his native town.

NOTES AND GLOSSARY:

bellezza: (*Italian*) beauty

Romance peoples: *diese Romanen* are the southern races whose languages (French, Italian, Provencal, Catalan, Rhaeto-Romanic, Sardinian and Dalmatian) all stem from Latin

Kronberg: built in Renaissance style, the castle of Kronborg (in Danish) stands at Elsinore (Helsingør), a seaport on the east coast of Zealand, 45 miles north of Copenhagen. The ghost of Hamlet's father tells him here of the murder

Part 6

Tonio, who had left home with derision in his heart, almost sobs to see the familiar, damp, grey town, where now everything seems so small. He recalls his dreams, in which his father had reproached his dissolute life—and Tonio feels his father was right.

At the hotel a gentleman in black cannot decide on Tonio's social category. In his room, after a night of confused dreams, he dresses himself with unusual care. He is glad of the mask of security that his work-worn face gives him, for he fears recognition.

As if still in his rueful dream, he visits the Market Square, Inge's house, the Millwall where he had walked with Hans, and, at last, the ancestral home. Almost expecting his father to appear, the 'son of the house' discovers his home is now the Public Library. He takes down a volume, that he knows well, and admires its artistry; but his thoughts are of his grandmother, his parents, his childhood and of the old walnut tree in the garden. He has seen enough and makes a clumsy exit.

He prepares to leave for Denmark, but Herr Seehaase, the fat little proprietor, whom he recognises, has summoned a policeman. They are looking for a criminal with a foreign name. Tonio, who has no papers, feels that—up to a point—they are right to interrogate him, and decides not to mention his father. Instead, he enjoys the effect, as they study his latest proof-sheets. Seehaase apologises and Tonio leaves his home-town.

NOTES AND GLOSSARY

Rathaus: the Town Hall, which epitomises the middle class virtues

Lindenplatz: 'the square of the lime trees'. Everywhere Tonio goes accurately reflects the town of Lübeck, and emphasises the autobiographical nature of the work

pious . . . motto: many German houses today preserve the tradition of a Christian inscription over the front door. The centuries-old maxim of the Kröger family is half-erased. It is a reminder of the days when words, for Tonio's forbears, were merely a means to express a pious lesson. Now the family is no longer there to restore the motto. It is a reminder, also, that Tonio has chosen to express his own thoughts in his own words, and has wandered far from the bourgeois family home

Public Library: with ironic artistry, Mann transforms Tonio's old home into a public library, a storehouse of literature for ordinary people. Here art and life have blended in a way that they have failed to in Tonio himself. Thus he is no longer at home here, and must go on his way. The volume he takes down and recognises so easily is probably one of his own works, for this would heighten the irony: Tonio's art can reach the public, but he himself cannot

Seehaase: this incident also has a factual basis, for in 1890 Thomas Mann was similarly questioned in error by the police

Part 7

On the deck in the moonlight, Tonio forgets both the interrogation and the poignant memories of childhood, losing himself in the darkness and the roar of the Baltic. A young Hamburg merchant artlessly, ecstatically, enthuses at the stars, feeling himself a mere worm beside them.

Tonio is sure he writes 'business-men's verses'. He tries to sleep but is sick and returns to the deck. Now the waves tower like licking flames. The tiger and the polar bear in the hold cry out in agony, and Tonio exults in the arrogance of the elements.

In the grey morning the Hamburger blushes at his poetic indiscretions. Tonio disembarks in Copenhagen and plays the role of the intelligent tourist, but the sounds and sights of the commonplace life fill him with a foolish, sweet restlessness, half memory, half hope, and so he leaves for Aarlsgaard in search of solitude.

NOTES AND GLOSSARY:

Plattdeutsch: a dialect of North Germany, less elegant than the conventional educated *Hochdeutsch*. Tonio is glad to hear it, for it belongs to 'the people', the everyday life

Bengal: the tiger comes from India, and the bear from the polar wilds. In them Tonio sees a splendid symbol of elemental life. Moreover, they are on their way to a menagerie, and again he must be reminded of the ordinary people who will enjoy seeing them

Kurhaus: a spa hotel

the merchant: his 'heavy sing-song accent' and his habit of spitting his consonants prove he is from Hamburg. Mrs Lowe-Porter's translation makes him speak less with an accent than with a cold, but it does no harm to the comedy

Copenhagen: the Danish Capital København means 'Merchant's harbour'. The very name heralds the bourgeois virtues that Tonio is seeking

the 'Horse': equestrian statue of Christian V (1646–99), popular absolute monarch of Denmark and Norway

Thorwaldsen: Bertel Thorwaldsen (1768–1844), a Danish sculptor much admired by Mann. He reinterpreted the ancient classical statues, and his religious masterpiece is *Christ and the Twelve Apostles* (1838) in the Vor Fru Kirke (Church of Our Lady) not far from the Nytorv or New Market and the Tivoli pleasure gardens

Part 8

Tonio breakfasts in a room overlooking the sea. He enjoys the peaceful mediocrity of his companions, a twittering landlady, an apopletic fish-dealer and three taciturn Americans with their tutor. Whether the sea is smooth and idle, charging like a bull, or just a sound in the distance, he loses himself in profound oblivion.

One day a miraculous sunrise over a shimmering sea proclaims the arrival of several families. Tonio anticipates their reunion with pleasure. Suddenly, calmly, the blonde Inge and the handsome, almost contemptuously confident Hans walk in, dressed as for Herr Knaak's dancing class.

Timorous but glad, Tonio lies alone in his darkened room until the waltz begins. Steadily he steals towards the music. A comic, 'provincial lion' officiously directs the cheerful, unaffected dancers. Joyfully Tonio sees Hans and Inge again—or rather, these representatives of the untroubled, aloof, simple blond and blue-eyed type.

Home-sick, Tonio recalls that he has never forgotten them. Now, though, he no longer wants Hans to read *Don Carlos*: free of the curse of knowledge, he and Inge must remain in blessed mediocrity. He envies them, knowing he himself could never be like this: such as he are doomed to go astray.

Tonio blushes at the memory evoked by a quadrille. He dares not approach Inge, for she would laugh at him again. Even if he were the greatest of artists she would laugh—and rightly, he feels. He longs for sleep—but the dance of life and art goes on . . .

A delicate girl with swimming black eyes, who alone has looked at him, trips and Tonio helps her up. Gently he bids her not to dance any more.

Jealous, exhausted, suffering, Tonio is still happy to be alive. Alone in his dark room again, he recalls the fevers and frosts of the hot senses and icy intellect that have made him an artist. Downstairs the waltz of life can still be heard.

NOTES AND GLOSSARY:

Aarlsgaard:	in September 1899 Mann felt in need of a holiday and went to the hotel at Aarlsgaard am Sund. A contemporary photograph of the hotel and of a typical bill are shown in *Bild und Text bei Thomas Mann* by H. Wysling and Y. Schmidtlin, Franke Verlag, Berne and Münich, 1975. Other photographs show Mann, his family, and his home town of Lübeck at the turn of the century
wurst:	(*German*) sausage
schinken:	(*German*) ham
Ingeborg and Hans:	the two dancers are symbols for Tonio, and not really the friends of his childhood. This is made quite clear later when Tonio says 'she was perhaps his sister'

Inge's laughter: the three men whose work Tonio mentions represent the highest artistic and intellectual achievements not just of Germany and Italy, the countries that have formed Tonio's personality, but of all mankind. To combine such musical, philosophical and painterly gifts with his own poetic accomplishment would require unsurpassed genius. Even so, Inge would not be impressed or understand, and Tonio feels this is as it should be. She represents something different, equally valid and very enviable —life

the nine symphonies: the Nine Symphonies of Ludwig van Beethoven, the German composer (1770–1827) are a sublime achievement. Beethoven was a major influence on Richard Wagner. Thomas Mann himself, like Tonio, admires Wagner's wild, awesome, deathly music, and borrows its 'leitmotif' technique (whereby familiar themes recur persistently) but ultimately, like Beethoven in his Ninth Symphony, both Mann and Tonio prefer love and joy in an affirmation of life

The World as Will and Idea: written in 1819 by Arthur Schopenhauer (1788–1860), a German philosopher who exerted great influence over Nietzsche, Wagner, and Mann himself. Profoundly pessimistic and determinist, he regards the world as irrational and a prey to the blind will, which one can at best quietly accept. There is still a place for private morality, for the good man will not seek to affect the workings of the will on other people. The artist who, like Tonio, withdraws from life must reveal to more practical people what they themselves cannot see

The Last Judgement: a painting executed between 1533 and 1541 by the Tuscan, Michelangelo Buonarroti-Simoni (1475–1564), the greatest sculptor since the ancient Greeks and a painter of genius. Pope Clement VII commissioned him in 1533 to decorate the Sistine Chapel. The painting, 44 ft × 48 ft, depicts Christ and the Virgin, the judgement of the damned, and the resurrection of the saved

sleep . . . : Tonio again quotes Theodor Storm's poem, but he is perhaps thinking once more of Hamlet as well. Worn out by thought, Hamlet contemplates suicide: '. . . To die; to sleep;/ No more; and by a sleep to say we end/The heartache and the thousand natural shocks/That flesh is heir to; 'tis a consummation/ Devoutly to be wished. To die; to sleep...' (*Hamlet*, III, 1, 56). Tonio's innate love of life would forbid such a course, but often the pain of real life makes him yearn to forget everything

Tak, O, mange tak!: the Danish girl, in thanking Tonio, reminds him of his youthful admirer, Magdalena Vermehren

---

Part 9

In a letter to Lisabeta, Tonio explains that he loves life precisely because he is, as she said, a '*bourgeois*'. His mixed parentage has made him into an artist with a guilt complex. Distrusting art, he yearns for respectability and normality.

Though he admires the cold pride of those daemonic artists who despise humanity, he prefers the warm, bourgeois love that alone produces poetry. With this love he will try to redeem the tragedy and comedy of life in his art; but his deepest love remains for the commonplace. It is a fruitful love—'There is longing in it, and a gentle envy; a touch of contempt and no little innocent bliss.'

NOTES AND GLOSSARY:

Arcady: Arcady or Arcadia, in the Peloponnese, is the Greek rural ideal. The story comes full circle, recalling the classical associations at the start. Lisabeta and Tonio's teacher both dwell in the rarified world of art and knowledge. Tonio 'will return' to the south, but meantime he needs to renew his contact with the clean, simple life of the north, 'if his art is to have meaning'

love: in the Bible, 1 Corinthians 13:1 and 2, St Paul writes: 'Though I speak with the tongues of men and of angels, and have not charity, I am become as sounding brass or a tinkling cymbal. And though I have the gift of prophecy, and understand all prophecies and all knowledge; and though I have all faith, so that I could remove mountains, and have not charity, I am nothing.' Tonio shares this view, for no matter how beautiful or how musical his words may sound, his literature can never rise to the level of poetry unless it is inspired by love of his fellow man. Without a love of life, his comments on life are 'nothing'

Part 3

Commentary

Artist and bourgeois

The story of *Tonio Kröger* hinges on the tense relationship between the creativity of the artist and the passive enjoyment of the average citizen. Within so wide a compass we find a myriad of types, some favouring one extreme and some the other. Sometimes a bourgeois strays out of his depth and makes a fool of himself, but others, such as Consul Kröger, are men with poetic leanings, who are far from foolish; even so, they flirt with danger, for imagination can undermine action. As Hamlet says, and Tonio would all too readily agree, 'Thus conscience doth make cowards of us all'—in other words, if you spend too long looking at problems, you lose the more instinctive urge to solve them. On the other hand, some 'bourgeois' people are so spontaneous and unthinking that they never even see there is a problem. In Irwin this is an unpleasant trait; in Inge it is the essence of her charm. Others still, like Hans, are immensely competent as well as charming, but even they require the stimulus of art if they are not to stagnate.

Much of the Novelle inevitably reflects Tonio's growing awareness of the nature of art itself. As a child he demonstrates acute powers of observation and clearly has great potential as an artist. Nevertheless, his earliest achievement is self-indulgent; later he will call it 'as good as nothing'. (p.191). This is because his work lacks a solid basis of warm human experience, without which it is insubstantial: mere pretty pictures. At this stage he totally rejects an emotional response to life: 'If you care too much about what you have to say, if your heart is too much in it, you can be pretty sure of making a mess.' (p.152). He adds that 'feeling, warm, heartfelt feeling is always banal and futile'. Above all he claims that the artist must be 'unhuman, extra-human', for 'The very gift of style, of form and expression, is nothing else than this cool and fastidious attitude towards humanity.' (p.152). Yet all these observations are really variants on his earlier dogmatic statement: 'one must die to life in order to be utterly a creator'. (p.149).

Now this is a very ambiguous observation. In one sense it is true, and Tonio never deviates: he believes that the artist must be absolutely truthful, and clinically impartial. His 'cool and fastidious style' is his gift to humanity, for he gives a coherent sense to otherwise shapeless lives. To this extent the artist 'dies to life'. Yet later Tonio will admit that without the original 'warm, heartfelt feeling' nothing fruitful will emerge. The artist must live life, and then, through the alchemy of his art, transmute it into broader philosophical lessons that will serve all men.

Until he has learnt this, Tonio shares with Hamlet a sense of weary, stale, flat and unprofitable meaninglessness: 'I tell you I am sick to death of depicting humanity without having any part or lot in it.' (p.153). Thus he concludes: 'Literature is not a calling, it is a curse.' (p.153). Those critics who find Tonio arrogantly conscious of his superiority and insultingly condescending to the less articulate are unjust. Of course he feels superior—'up to a point'—for he has a rare gift. Yet the agony he endures is related with candour, and he genuinely feels that the average person has an equally valuable gift—the ability to live.

Tonio cries bitterly to Lisabeta: 'Not to let the sadness of the world unman you; to read, mark, learn and put to account even the most torturing things and to be of perpetual good cheer in the sublime consciousness of moral superiority over the horrible invention of existence —yes, thank you!' (p.157). In his ironic disclaimer he seems to reject the role of the artist. Some see in this mere hypocrisy. They feel that Mann is simply glamourising the artist by exaggerating his difficulties. Again, this is unjust. Mann is not falsely modest; he has a rare calling, and is not so dishonest as to deny it. The artist can quite reasonably lay claim to 'moral superiority' in that he can help the less visionary to find their way in life to higher ideals. Yet the tone of the whole speech again makes it clear that Tonio is profoundly unhappy in much of his daily life. He does not strike a pose, he gives a balanced view.

His contempt for the 'small fry', to whom talent is just another 'social asset' (p.148) is quite reasonable in a man who suffers so keenly for his calling. Moreover, if at first he despises the dilettanti, by the end he accepts even them in his all-embracing love of humanity. The arrogance fades, but not so the validity of his view of art as a most demanding master.

When Tonio exclaims: 'No problem, none in the world, is more tormenting than that of the artist and his human aspect' (p.155) we may be tempted to smile and add 'more tormenting to you, Tonio', and then we could not disagree. At first glance, though, as it stands, it seems a sweeping overstatement in a world marred by war, famine, intolerance and disease. Yet men need someone to find a pattern in the sometimes seemingly pointless confusion of life. In that sense Tonio is right: the artist, tortured by what he sees, must remain above the fray. Only in preserving his artistic integrity, often at terrible personal cost, can he be the consolation of those he serves.

Characterisation

Tonio is the focal point of the story, and every character who impinges upon his life in some way reflects an aspect of his own personality. In effect, everyone lives on two levels: firstly as a character in his or her own right, and secondly as a symbol of the conflict in Tonio's soul. Similarly, every description of Tonio himself brings out the essential dichotomy between his love of life and his love of art. Thus Tonio himself is both an individual and a representative type.

Tonio Kröger's physical appearance

Tonio's main physical feature is his Mediterranean looks. His appearance reflects his artistic temperament, for spiritually he at first inclines towards the free, sunny, creative artistry of the Italians: 'While beneath Tonio's round fur cap was a brunette face with the finely chiselled features of the south: the dark eyes with delicate shadows and too heavy lids looked dreamily and a little timorously on the world.' (p.130). Unlike the confident, elastic gait of the blue-eyed 'commonplace' people: 'Tonio's walk was idle and uneven' (p.130) and his uneasiness is heralded by his stance: 'He gazed into space with his head on one side. Posture and manner were habitual' (p.130).

His face, his gait and his drooping head become a *leitmotif* that instantly signals his painful sense of inadequacy. At the dance he recalls Storm's poem with 'bent head and gloomy brows' (p.142). Yet the memory of Inge fades and he goes upon his inevitable artistic way: '... a little idly, a little irregularly, whistling to himself, gazing into space with his head on one side; and if he went wrong, it is because for some people there is no such thing as a right way.' (p.146).

His early success as an artist makes him still more remote from the common people, for until Lisabeta recalls him to his beginnings, he simply despises them; and this marks his very expression: '... because he could not endure the blithe and innocent with their darkened understanding, while they in turn were troubled by the sign on his brow.' (p.147).

The conversation with Lisabeta is crucial in his development, for from it he recovers his appreciation of his bourgeois origins. This is strongly reinforced by the formality of his appearance and his behaviour. On seeing her: 'He ... bowed with some ceremony, although Lisabeta Ivanovna was a good friend.' (p.149). She bids him be less 'formal' and jokes that: 'Everybody knows you were taught good manners in your nursery.' (p.149). She chuckles too at his 'aristocratic garments': 'His dress, reserved in cut and a soothing shade of grey was punctilious and dignified to the last degree.' (p.150).

Again Mann draws attention to his frown and to the 'severe correctness of his parting'. Though the 'gentle mouth and chin' recall his maternal tendencies, the memory of his father is proclaimed already in his formal appearance. Symbolically he 'covered his eyes and brow', for the conflict of north and south, of fixative and the breath of spring, is at a crisis.

When the crisis has passed, and he is reconciled both to his bourgeois origins and his artistic leanings, he says: 'Thank you, Lisabeta Ivanovna. Now I can go home in peace. I am expressed.' (p.161). It is significant that he leaves 'resolutely' and takes his hat and stick, the trappings of a 'Bürger', for his new found briskness reflects his calm of mind. Perhaps this is why Lisabeta jokingly calls him 'little Father', for the endearment underlines the profound truth that His 'Highness', the aloof artist, can now indeed return to the home of his fathers.

With 'his head inclined against the wind'—a more positive variant on his usual drooping posture—he returns home. Looking down at the 'medieval city' from a room in 'patriarchal style'—phrases that emphasise the traditions in which Tonio is steeped—he whistles and frowns, and in the hotel register 'Tonio, his head on one side, scrawled something . . . that might be taken for a name, a station, a place of origin'. The setting and the stance recall the little boy who wished to become a famous writer; but now he merely scribbles anonymously, and for the moment art and words matter much less than his redis-covered love of his father's values. No wonder this too is expressed physically, as he observes the 'plump fair-haired populace': '. . . and a nervous laugh mounted in him, mysteriously akin to a sob.' (p.163).

Symbolically, also, the climate offers 'already a hint of autumn' (p.165), in contrast to the 'air of art, the tepid, sweet air of permanent spring' (p.148), and in this bracing atmosphere Tonio spends 'more care than usual on his toilette'. The influence of his father is now explicit: 'as though about to call upon some smart family where a well-dressed and flawless appearance was *de rigueur*; and while occupied in this wise he listened to the anxious beating of his heart.' (p.165). The rebirth of love lights up Tonio's face: 'The muscles of his face relaxed, and he looked at men and things with a look grown suddenly calm.' (p.166). Satisfied, he can go north to Denmark, though as an artist he remains an object of suspicion. He watches the loading of the cargo: '. . . as he used to do as a boy with his father.' (p.173). In the spiritual presence of his father he sails for Elsinor, where Hamlet before him had to recon-cile his love of his father's memory with his love of a mother of whom he could not approve. Now enfolded in the might of the Baltic: 'he bent his head to the strong salt wind.' (p.173).

Here the gesture is almost religious, recalling his earlier obeisance before the flame on the altar of love. His love of Ingeborg Holm herself, though, was ephemeral, whereas now Tonio, standing in the gathering darkness, feels an immense sense of peace beyond space and time.

This ideal state cannot be more than a goal, of course. Life has to be lived as it is, and in the streets of Denmark Tonio suffers keenly from his continuing sense of isolation. Now, though, he knows he can help those whom he loves, but who reject him. All the physical details symbolically contrast with his own appearance again. Surrounded by fair hair and blue eyes, he repined 'after the lost and gone' and 'a sudden laugh would pierce him to his marrow' (p.177), as Ingeborg Holm's laugh had long ago.

More purposeful now, Tonio looks at the sea, 'das Erlebnis der Ewigkeit, des Nichts und des Todes, ein metaphysischer Traum' ('that experience of eternity, of nothingness, and of death, a metaphysical dream'), or, in Professor Wilkinson's fine words, 'the solace for all who have seen too deep into the complexity of things'.* Again his face reflects his mood: 'it called, it lured, it beckoned him. And he smiled.' (p.179).

Significantly, he now takes an active, healthy part in life. He goes for walks and swims in the sea, immersing himself physically in a 'joyous daze' in this symbol of 'joyous oblivion'. Equally pointed is his initial reaction to Magdalena's Danish counterpart: 'He turned away . . .' (p.186). She is not even given a name, for we see everything through Tonio's eyes and to him she is just a Danish girl who has, like himself, taken the wrong path. Hans and Inge are suitable names for the other Danes, for they are mere types of the lucky unthinking commonplace, to whom Tonio invariably turns and returns. Much of the book in fact shows him getting up and going away, for he knows he cannot belong, and he must seek his path, even if it is bound to be a wrong one.

Again his physical reaction is to 'sob with nostalgia and remorse', alone in his room while others dance. After all, his eternal symbolic posture is expressed in his letter to Lisabeta: 'I stand between two worlds, I am at home in neither . . .' (p.190); and yet his deepest love remains for the 'blond and blue-eyed', so different from himself, but who unwittingly contribute so much to his art and his bliss.

Tonio's artistic propensities

Tonio is a spectator in the theatre of life, never invited to perform, but even so a lynx-eyed critic, whose observations can help the actors better to interpret their given roles. Words are his consolation. Mentally or physically he notes down all he sees. His insight often pains him, but only such unflinching honesty of vision can disentangle the shapelessness in the lives of those he serves, whilst giving meaning to his own.

Sometimes the words are too deeply felt to be uttered: 'Tonio did not

*Tonio Kröger, Oxford, 1968, p.xlv.

speak. He suffered.' (p.130). Yet his heart leaps when: 'he saw Hans was sorry for his remissness.' (p.131).

Throughout the story verbs of observation underline Tonio's instinctive need to record what he sees. Whereas the blue eyes of the fair-haired Hans and his millions of counterparts gaze beautifully and unseeingly upon the world, content just to be seen and admired, the brown eyes of the race of the artistic ones see all too clearly, even when they would rather not.

Tonio personifies such people: 'he was so organised that he received such experiences consciously, wrote them down as it were internally, and even, in a certain way, took pleasure in them.' (p.131). This very clearly anticipates the end of the story. Even as a child Tonio rises above his personal misery and draws a general conclusion from a particular instance. Of course this does not stop the suffering, but it enriches his life. As an adult he will achieve a far greater degree of philosophical detachment, take a still keener pleasure in shaping the events around him, and for all his isolation still feel a profound joy. In the 'prose ballad' of the Novelle the cello's melancholy tones predominate, but the conclusion hints at the soaring violins that will soon take up Tonio's theme.

Tonio is so built that: '. . . during his lessons in the vaulted Gothic classrooms he was mainly occupied in feeling his way about among these intuitions of his and penetrating them.' (p.131). Even though he half approves of his schoolmates and masters for their own disapproval of him, he has no illusions about them: 'in his turn (with extraordinary penetration) saw through them and disliked their personal weaknesses and bad feeling.' (p.132). These unusual powers of observation in fact win Hans's admiration: 'Hans respected Tonio's superior power of putting certain difficult matters into words.' (p.134). Again, there is a strong hint that the bourgeois need the artist as much as he needs them.

When Hans sides with Irwin and ridicules Tonio's hybrid name, again Tonio understands all too clearly his own isolation: 'How it hurt to have to see through all this!' (p.137). The irony is particularly bitter to him, since the names of things mean so much to him. A happier irony occurs when he falls in love with Inge. He foresees pain and joy, which will be no good to him: 'because he would never have the time or tranquillity to give them permanent form.' (p.139). Indeed he feels this so forcibly that the phrase reappears at once: 'he longed to be vital and rich, far more than he did to work tranquilly on anything to give it permanent form.' (p.139).

As an artist he later proves that he can work like this, and even if the pain of love endures, his life does indeed become 'vital and rich'. As a child, though, the agony is so great that at times he cannot even bear to look at life, for he always sees too much. He gazes 'through the blind' at Inge's, a spectator at the drama of his own life: 'For he was looking within, into himself, the theatre of so much pain and longing.' (p.143). Yet even when he dares not look, he yearns to *hear* as exactly as possible: '. . . even although he stood lonely and aloof, seeking to distinguish the warm notes of her voice amid the buzzing, clattering and laughter within.' (p.143).

All the time, however, his artistic need to organise his emotions is preparing the way for his ultimate acceptance of his lot. When he deduces from his experience at the dancing-class that 'happiness is in loving, not in being loved', he emerges a profoundly wiser boy: 'And he took inward note of this thought, wrote it down in his mind; followed out all its implications and felt it to the depths of his soul.' (p.145).

This essential theme of 'looking' develops unhappily into that of 'looking down'. Tonio loses sight of his roots, to which he owes his energy and moral strength. He rejects all that is good in them: '. . . he looked down on the lowly and vulgar life he had led so long in these surroundings.' (p.146). Now a rather unpleasant arrogance colours his thoughts. He surrenders to the power of Art, 'to whose service he felt called': though his surrender is almost a religious experience, and his vocation is unquestionably sincere, the grandeur of the phrase matches his haughty consciousness of his superiority over the common people. He yields to 'the power of intellect, the power of the word, that lords it with a smile over the unconscious and inarticulate.' (p.147). Later he will temper the tone of these remarks, though he never denies their essential truth. What will change is his attitude towards those less articulate than himself.

In his search for the right word, Tonio's vision grows ever keener. He rejects empty pomposity: 'It sharpened his eyes and made him see through the large words which puff out the bosoms of mankind.' (p.147). He sees the true value of things: '. . . it opened for him men's souls and his own, made him clairvoyant, showed him the inwardness of the world, and the ultimate behind men's words and deeds.' (p.147). Above all, he puts it in words that anticipate his eventual promise in the letter to Lisabeta: 'And all that he saw could be put into two words: the comedy and the tragedy of life.' (p.147). Now he looks down on the 'tragic and laughable figures' but later (p.191) he will look up to them again and wish to redeem them.

For a time his 'love of form' and the 'pleasures of expression' make his life 'sweeter and sweeter'. Yet there is a real danger that, like von Aschenbach in *Tod in Venedig* (*Death in Venice*), he will lose all sense of morality in his quest for perfect form. For Aschenbach the lovely Tadzio heralds death. Tonio, however, though he has temporarily forgotten it, is a Kröger, and the Kröger moral values counterbalance the licentious behaviour that produces his artistry. His 'icy intellect and scorching sense' combine to create an excess 'which at bottom he despised' (p.148). Though he is 'rasped by the banal', and though Mann writes of 'the irritable fastidiousness of his taste', Tonio achieves great art only because his intellect and his senses are fortified by immense industry. And this literary manifestation of Nietzsche's Will to Power he owes mainly to the blood of his father's family.

This blood prickles with the coming of spring. His contempt for the inarticulate will never entirely fade—it endures to the very last line of the story—but already it is softened by his growing awareness that he still reveres such ordinary mortals. He says of the Spring to Lisabeta '. . . I don't succeed in looking down on it; for the truth is it makes me feel ashamed; I quail before its sheer naturalness and triumphant youth.' (p.152). Lisabeta shrewdly discerns the rebirth of Tonio's love of the commonplace. When he inveighs against the conditions of the artist's life, she interjects with tender irony: 'Observed, Tonio Kröger? If I may ask, only "observed"?' (p.156). She has noticed, as the reader does too, that Tonio is no mere camera, clinically recording all he sees. The feelings Tonio has sought to subjugate are ever present in him, and soon he will openly acknowledge them with a sob of nostalgia and remorse. She defends the positive function of the artist in very revealing terms: '. . . simply by reminding you of some things you very well know yourself.' (p.156).

Tonio's 'good friend' really is a friend and knows him better than he knows himself. She emphasises the 'purifying and healing influence of letters', and these words are redolent of the spirit of Tonio's subsequent letter to her. She speaks of 'the subduing of the passions by knowledge and eloquence', which has been a feature of Tonio's character since childhood. She speaks then of: 'literature as the guide to understanding, forgiveness and love, the redeeming power of the word, literary art as the highest manifestation of the human mind, the poet as the most highly developed of human beings, the poet as saint.' (p.156). Gently she recalls Tonio to a sense of purpose. She is a Russian, and Tonio acknowledges that her compatriots—one thinks of Turgenev,* Dostoyevsky† and Tolstoy‡ among many—have indeed shown these uplifting qualities. Lisabeta speaks, then, with a symbolic authority and her words echo the thoughts of St Paul. Later Tonio will quote directly from Paul's message of love, without which the writer or indeed any-

---

*Ivan Turgenev (1818–83), the first Russian writer of the nineteenth century to acquire an international reputation. His masterpiece is his novel *Fathers and Sons* (1862).

†Fyodor Dostoyevsky (1821–81) the Russian novelist, whose works include *Crime and Punishment* (1866) and *The Brothers Karamazov* (1879–80).

‡Leo Tolstoy (1828–1910), the major Russian novelist, whose masterpieces are *War and Peace* (1865–69) and *Anna Karenina* (1875–77).

body is 'nothing'. Tonio's conversation with Lisabeta is his confession, from which he emerges shriven and whole again. He has rediscovered his lost morality. When he admits that one can almost 'worship' the Russian authors, he consciously emphasises the moral responsibility of the artist.

The spasms of anguish that follow are merely the brief contractions of a disease that has been conquered. Tonio is effectively cured even when he exclaims: 'To see things clear, if even through your tears, to recognise, notice, observe—and have to put it all down with a smile, at the very moment when hands are clinging, and lips meeting, and the human gaze is blinded with feeling—it is infamous.' (p.157). The image is startling, for one cannot 'see' if one is 'blind', but Tonio, as we know, sees things inwardly. Now, though, he acknowledges that he has never truly ceased to feel sympathy for commonplace life. He suffers still, but his art is now acquiring a moral purpose.

Tonio knows that his role will continue to bring him pain, for often an artist is mocked for what appears to be stupidity, but is in fact only the arrogance and timidity of a reserved and sceptical man. Nevertheless, for the first time he confesses to another human being: 'I love life.' (p.158).

He looks at the table in his hotel room 'with absent eyes' (p.169), as he broods on his visit to the Library. The moment recalls the unhappy child at the dancing class. The compensations of his vision are at hand, however. During the voyage he enjoys the romantic extravagances of the business-man, which before he would have despised: 'Tonio Kröger listed to all this engaging artlessness and was privately drawn to it.' (p.175). Most tellingly, when he listens to the roar of the waves and of the caged animals in the hold, he starts to apostrophise the sea: 'O thou wild friend of my youth. Once more I behold thee . . .' (p.176). His heart, however, is too full to crystallise his thoughts in a poem. 'It was not fated to receive a final form or in tranquillity to be welded to a perfect whole.' (p.176). The phrases recall his feelings when he fell in love with Inge. Again life sweeps aside his art, but not forever. Soon they will dwell in harmony. For the moment, though, the flame of love, stifled so long beneath the ashes, blazes forth the more brilliantly.

In Denmark he goes through the motions of a cultivated tourist intent on 'improving his mind' (p.177). He studies the great Danish art treasures: 'But all this is not exactly what he saw.' (p.177). What he actually sees lies deeper. He sees that the great artists of Denmark such as Thorwaldsen have enriched the lives of the people. Their work, appropriately, is in the Market and the Church and the Pleasure Gardens. As in the Public Library that used to be his home, he sees how the artist can serve the community and help men to aspire to loftier ideals.

Now the words he hears and the sights he sees everywhere remind him of this. In the syllables of the names he hears an 'accent of plaintive reproach'. 'He walked, he gazed, drawing deep, lingering draughts of moist sea air; and everywhere he saw eyes as blue, hair as blond, faces as familiar, as those that had visited his rueful dreams the night he had spent in his native town.' (p.177). Now his artistic sense is invigorated by the fresh air of life.

And so he goes to Elsinore, in the steps of 'that typical literary man', Hamlet the Dane. To Lisabeta he had cried: 'He knew what it meant to be called to knowledge without being born to it. To see things clear, if even through your tears, . . . it is infamous, Lisabeta, it is indecent, out-rageous . . . but what good does it do to be outraged?' (p.157). Now, though, he can cope with his problem, for despite the pain he no longer feels a sense of outrage. At peace, now, he knows that, like Thorwaldsen, he has much to offer those he loves, and is glad. He no longer needs Horatio's warning that ''Twere to consider too curiously, to consider so' (p.156) for, thanks to his father's influence, he has the strength of character to look honestly at things and not to flinch from the conse-quences. And thanks to his mother's influence, he can turn these things to the public profit through the medium of his art.

Even so, there will always be tears for Tonio. Sobbing in his room, as the Danes dance happily below, he reflects on artistic creation and feels: 'ravaged and paralysed by insight, half worn out by the fevers and frosts of creation.' (p.189). He is at his lowest ebb. 'Erring, forsaken, martyred and ill' are all epithets that state that he is not only unhappy, but the victim of a force too strong for him, that has led him the wrong way. Yet this is not the final word.

His letter to Lisabeta is written in a calmer frame of mind and more truly expresses his considered, balanced view. At times, he admits the pull of life is stronger than that of art: 'Sometimes now I have days when I would rather state things in general terms than go on telling stories.' (p.189). This is a big admission from one who describes things in their minutest detail. He even calls himself: 'an artist with a bad conscience' (p.190). Ultimately, however, he will not forsake his art. Not only is it part of him, but it enables him to 'redeem the tragic and the laughable', whose world needs shaping. His art lets him serve those he loves.

Tonio's bourgeois propensities

'Consul Kröger's son' learns from his shrewd friend Lisabeta that he is a 'bourgeois manqué' (p.161). Eventually he not only accepts the statement, but justifies it, writing to her: 'You adorers of the beautiful, who call me phlegmatic and without aspirations, you ought to realise that there is a way of being an artist that goes so deep and is so much a matter of origins and destinies that no longing seems to it sweeter and more worth knowing than longing after the bliss of the commonplace.' (p.190). At the end of the story he wishes only to put his art to the service of his 'deepest and secretest love': 'the blond and blue-eyed, the fair and the living, the happy, lovely and commonplace.' (p.191). This has come about precisely because his bourgeois origins have given him the strength of purpose and the moral integrity that a fruitful artist requires.

With delicate irony Thomas Mann smiles at Tonio's frantic efforts to free himself from his bourgeois shackles and to become an artist; for it is only when he finally yields to his own bourgeois instincts that Tonio can actually become the great artist he wishes to be. The signs are clear on every page of the Novelle.

Even as a schoolboy he has a grudging sympathy for the bourgeois point of view: 'But then, on the other hand, he himself felt his verse-making extravagant and out of place and to a certain extent agreed with those who considered it an unpleasing occupation.' (p.132).

He shows a similar attitude towards his parents: 'Though at the same time he found his father's annoyance a more dignified and respectable attitude and despite his scoldings understood him very well, whereas his mother's blithe indifference always seemed just a little wanton.' (p.132). As ever, the rather apologetic qualifications emphasise his divided state of mind.

In a famous passage, that runs as a refrain throughout his thoughts, he reflects: 'After all we are not gypsies living in a green wagon; we're respectable people, the family of Consul Kröger.' (p.133). Even so, his very name reminds him that he is 'different . . .like a stranger among the other boys' (p.137). Much as he loves Hans, the archetypal bourgeois in miniature, Tonio: '. . . made no attempt to be like Hans Hansen, perhaps hardly ever seriously wanted to.' (p.134). All he wants is to be loved in return. Tonio cannot be like Hans, if he is to be an imaginative artist; but his love of Hans already anticipates the conclusion of the Novelle. Likewise, his love of Inge anticipates the selfless nature of his future artistry: '. . . his soul embraced thy blonde, simple, pert, commonplace little personality in blissful self-abnegation.' (p.144).

Even when he goes his artistic way, Tonio betrays his bourgeois leanings. On his mother's remarriage: 'Tonio Kröger found this a little irregular, but who was he to call her to order, who wrote poetry himself and could not even give an answer when asked what he meant to do in life?' (p.146). His own excesses disgust him: 'It might have been his father in him, that tall, thoughtful fastidiously dressed man with the wild flower in his buttonhole, that made him suffer so down there.' (p.147). He exclaims again: 'As though I had a wagonful of travelling gypsies for my ancestors!' (p.148). His elegant clothes underline the point. Moreover, he himself distrusts artists with the scornful suspicion: '. . . that my upright old forbears there on the Baltic would have felt for any juggler or mountebank that entered their houses.' (p.155).

He confesses to Lisabeta that he admires not the wild, daemonic, satanic excesses of an amoral Caesar Borgia. No, he loves '. . . life in all its seductive banality . . . the gnawing, surreptitious hankering, Lisabeta, for the bliss of the commonplace.' (p.159). He is certainly 'a bourgeois on the wrong path', but she points the way to a better one—to his home. Yet even now Tonio has not fully learned his lesson. Revoking the wishes of his childhood, he says that one should not '. . . tempt people to read poetry who would much rather read books about the instantaneous photography of horses.' (p.160).

At this turning point in his life, Tonio is too extreme. His refound love of bourgeois life brings in its train a rejection of his art: 'I'm fed up with Italy, I spew it out of my mouth. It's a long time since I imagined I could belong down there. Art, eh? . . . I decline with thanks.' (p.161). Later, he will want to return to Lisabeta 'down there in Arcady' (p.191) and a proper balance between the poles of art and life will be achieved.

The amusing scene with the gentleman in black puts Tonio's predicament in sharp focus. This artist who has abandoned his art for 'life' is such an enigma that the doorman cannot decide on Tonio's 'proper category, socially and hierarchically speaking' (p.164).

His various experiences in Lübeck and Denmark are recalled: '. . . with a sweet and timorous gladness such as he had not felt through all these long dead years.' (p.182). 'Dead' clearly states that his art has till now been sterile; the invigorating breath of bourgeois life will animate it and make it fruitful. He thinks of Adalbert in his café, escaping from life into an artificial limbo, and shrugs his shoulders. He prefers real life now, with whatever pain it may bring.

Much pain awaits him very soon: ' "Had I forgotten you?" he asked. "No never, Not thee, Hans, not thee Inge the fair. It was always you I worked for." ' (p.185). He wonders if it can ever change: 'To be like you! . . . Begin again? But it would be no good. It would turn out the same—everything would turn out the same as it did before.' (p.185). He knows that he is doomed to follow his artistic calling; for people like himself 'there is no such thing as a right path'. To an extent he is correct, for Tonio is indeed 'called to art'; it is a vocation he simply must obey. Yet it is not really a 'wrong path', for he will achieve so much for so many. Sadly though, with his nature, Tonio remains a stranger to those he loves.

When later he whispers the names of Hans and Inge into his pillow, they symbolise his 'true and native way of love'. To him the blue-eyed fair-haired ones mean 'life and home, . . . simple and heartfelt feeling' (p.189). Now he is certain: '. . . how much my love of life is one and the same thing as my being a bourgeois.' (p.190).

The story has indeed come full circle. Tonio the writer gratefully recognises his debt to his native town. And there, for him, the tale stops. For Thomas Mann himself the story had a happier ending. With the Freedom of Lübeck Hans and Inge at last requited his love.

Tonio's father

Consul Kröger is always present in the spirit, if not the flesh. The epitome of the Bürger's ideals of industry, integrity and decency, he gives Tonio what he himself has gained from his forefathers—the will to carry a task through to the end, allied to a firm sense of morality. Moreover, we must not confuse him with the Hansen type, for he is a thoughtful man who has, after all, married a most unusual bride. The artistic tendencies that flower in Tonio are germinating already in his father. As in *Buddenbrooks* the seeds of destruction are already sown for the family business. Yet Tonio does not die prematurely like the infant prodigy Hanno, for the spirit of his paternal ancestors recalls him sufficiently to reality for him to live a fruitful if lonely artistic life.

The 'tall, fastidiously dressed' man has the appearance and rank of a 'Bürger'; but his blue eyes are 'thoughtful', and the wild flower in his buttonhole is a hint of his leanings towards the wanton world from which he has chosen his wife. Even so, he is essentially bourgeois, and inevitably sends his son to dancing-classes in Frau Consul Hustede's drawing-room; for it is here that the 'first families' (p.140) send their children.

Even in death Tonio's father exerts a puritanical influence: 'The old Kröger family gradually declined, and some people quite rightly considered Tonio's existence and way of life as one of the signs of decay.' (p.146). 'Quite rightly' reflects Tonio's own suspicion of the artistic temperament.

To Lisabeta Tonio admits his debt: 'I suppose I must have inherited this northern tendency from my father, for my mother was really more for the *bellezza*, in so far that is as she cared very much one way or the other.' (p.162).

In his dreams in Lübeck his father reproaches him for his past excesses and Tonio feels only that this is 'as it should be' (p.164). His bourgeois conscience strikes again as he returns home: 'His heart gave a throb of fear, lest his father might come out of one of the doors on the ground floor, in his office coat, with his pen behind his ear, and take him to task for his excesses. He would have found the reproach quite in order.' (p.167). Now his father is recalled as '. . . that tall, correct, slightly melancholy and pensive gentleman with a wild flower in his buttonhole . . .' (p.168). 'Melancholy' now joins the familiar description, and we sense a new sympathy in Tonio. He is beginning to see his father as a fellow sufferer, tempted towards a more poetic world, and no longer a mere aloof, reproving gentleman.

When he last speaks of his father, in the letter to Lisabeta, Tonio has achieved stability. This is reflected in his description: 'My father, you know, had the temperament of the north: solid, reflective, puritanically correct, with a tendency to melancholia.' (p.190).

He is no longer a mere type, characterised by a leitmotif of blue eyes, smart dress and a wild flower. He is a man of bourgeois values with a propensity to look more deeply into things than most of his kind. He is a human being, full of contradictions, whom Tonio can remember with love and at last understand.

Tonio's mother

'But for his mother, she cared nothing about the reports—Tonio's beautiful black-haired mother, whose name was Consuelo, and who was so absolutely different from the other ladies in the town, because father had brought her long ago from some place far down on the map.' (p.132).

Consuelo has the name and looks and above all temperament of a southern race. The vagueness of 'long ago' and 'from some place' lend her a romantic mystery. She is 'dark', and the theme of the artistic nature is echoed; she is 'fiery', is wonderfully musical, and blithely indifferent. To the somewhat puritanical Tonio, no wonder she seems 'just a little wanton'.

He loves her deeply, but amid the company of his bourgeois friends he adds an apologetic disclaimer, in his plaintive efforts to win their approval: 'She comes from down there, you know . . .' (p.136). On her husband's death: 'Tonio's mother, his beautiful, fiery mother who played the piano and mandoline so wonderfully and to whom nothing mattered at all, she married again after a year's time.' (p.146). The gypsy wagon leaps to mind when we read this. Her music categorises her clearly among the artists, and with this goes an irresponsible *laisser faire* that contravenes Tonio's innate moral sense. The speed of her second marriage, moreover, strikes a chord, for Hamlet, 'that typical literary man', had seen his mother marry his uncle with equally unseemly haste. Furthermore, Tonio's stepfather epitomises all those characteristics that Tonio finds doubtful, for Consuelo Kröger '. . . married a musician, moreover, a virtuoso with an Italian name, and went away with him into remote blue distances.' (p.146). Thus they vanish literally into the blue, a colour which in this context paradoxically signifies the exotic, the fanciful, the romantic, with its suggestion of mountains blending with the horizon. Tonio symbolically follows her path. 'He lived in large cities and in the south, promising himself a luxuriant ripening of his art by southern suns; perhaps it was the blood of his mother's race that drew him thither.' (p.147).

When he returns to the north he can take stock and achieve a calmer, more balanced synthesis. Thus he writes to Lisabeta with the same sensible detachment that characterises his summary of his father in the same paragraph: 'My mother, of indeterminate foreign blood, was beautiful, sensuous, naïve, passionate and careless at once, and, I think, irregular by instinct.' (p.190). He can look with uncommon objectivity at the 'extraordinary dangers' that face the offspring of parents as contrasting as his own. The romantic leitmotifs are now omitted from Consuelo's description, for Tonio has looked beneath the symbol to the real person again, and, as with his father, loves her for what she was. Now he can see himself also for what he is: 'a bohemian who feels a nostalgic yearning for respectability'. His self-knowledge is the basis from which his artistry can redeem his fellows.

Hans

'Hans wore a Danish sailor cap with black ribbons, beneath which streamed a shock of straw-coloured hair. He was uncommonly handsome and well-built, broad in the shoulders and narrow in the hips with keen, far apart, steel-blue eyes.' (p.130). The contrast with Tonio is total. Hans represents the confident youth of the Lübeck Bürger (bourgeois) class, and his attractive Nordic appearance is, by force of repetition, firmly established as a symbol. His hair and eyes are the most immediately striking features of a child in whom Tonio idealises a way of life and a set of values.

Even his gait expresses his easy confidence: in contrast to Tonio his 'slim legs in their black stockings moved with an elastic rhythmic tread.' (p.130). He lives 'in the sunshine of popularity' and people say to him: 'Ah, here you are, Hans Hansen, with your pretty blond hair! Still head of the school? Remember me to your father and mother, there's a fine lad!' (p.133). Fair hair and his parentage form a persistent refrain, again firmly establishing a symbolic link. In Tonio's heartfelt question, the blue eyes emphasise the point: 'Who else has blue eyes like yours, or lives in such friendliness and harmony with all the world?' (p.133).

His people are prominent business men of consequence in the town, owners of the big wood yards by the river for many generations. Hans will clearly continue the tradition in his confident way. Already he is rather lordly and dogmatic: 'He had a spoilt and arbitrary way of announcing his likes and dislikes.' (p.137).

The trouble with Hans, and all those people he stands for, is that they are complacent, and this breeds over-confidence. Their lives become ·too comfortable and they prefer not to change. In other words, they cease to think of how life can be made better for others. Young Tonio knows that Hans must never be like himself: 'But it would do him no harm to read *Don Carlos* . . .' (p.138). This mild observation by a little boy contains a profound truth. The bourgeois class can only benefit from contact with art. They need the stimulus of brighter minds, if they are not to stagnate in a smug, amoral society.

Years later Hans's adult counterpart walks into the dance hall. He looks like Hans and is even in naval uniform—though a real one this time. Again we read of the broad shoulders and narrow hips. Yet he is not Hans. He is of the same race and type: 'This was the blond-fair-haired breed of the steel blue eyes, which stood to him for the pure, the blithe, the untroubled in life: for a virginal aloofness that was at once both simple and full of pride . . .' (p.184). Again Tonio admires such 'blessed mediocrity' and no longer wishes him to read *Don Carlos*: 'You must not cloud your clear eyes or make them dreamy and dim by peering into melancholy poetry . . .' (p.185).

Fortunately the mood passes. When he writes to Lisabeta he promises to redeem the 'tragic and the laughable figures'. There can be no doubt that he will write not just for the misfits in life, but also for those who are happy and lovely. Even if they may not actually read his work, what he has to say will inevitably affect them too, for they will be happy in a better world. With luck they may also read his work—it would do them 'no harm'.

Ingeborg

'Ingeborg Holm, blonde little Inge . . . the thick blonde plait, the longish, laughing blue eyes, the saddle of freckles . . . the commonplace phrase.' (p.139). She embodies all the beauty, the confidence and the unthinking attitudes of Hans. Tonio admires her 'narrow blue eyes full of fun and mockery' (p.139), as she trips hand in hand with Ferdinand Matthiessen. Again the fair hair, blue eyes and elastic tread symbolise a whole attitude of mind. Tonio laments the huge gulf between them: 'Oh lovely Inge, blonde Inge of the narrow laughing blue eyes! So lovely and laughing as you are one can only be if one does not read *Immensee* and never tries to write things like it. And that was just the tragedy!' (p.143). Yet this is not strictly true. Thomas Mann found in Katja a lovely girl who did use her brain! To this extent Tonio remains an individual, forever cut off from those he idolises. When the latter-day Inge's sleeve falls away from her elbow, Tonio feels a pang that, we sense, he will feel in a hundred different incidents still to come. That is his tragedy.

Magdalena

Her 'great dark brilliant eyes' and her 'drooping head' immediately show her to be Tonio's spiritual sister. No wonder she loves verse; still less that 'she often fell down in the dance'—in the dance of life, for which she is so ill-equipped.

Tonio's reactions to her and to her Danish counterpart significantly reflect the change in him. As a child he turned away from her; but as an adult, when the girl falls, he gently picks her up and recognises a fellow sufferer. The bourgeois good manners are more than mere form: they reflect the love he feels for all mankind.

Lisabeta

In many ways Lisabeta Ivanovna resembles Tonio too: 'Her brown hair, compactly dressed, already a little grey at the sides, was parted in the middle and waved over the temples, framing a sensitive, sympathetic, dark-skinned face, which was Slavic in its facial structure, with flat nose, strongly accentuated cheekbones and little bright, black eyes.' (p.150). And of course she too is an artist. Moreover, her Russian ancestry in itself suggests the deeply spiritual writers of that distant land.

There is, however, a positive, down-to-earth quality about her that merits her introductory description as 'a good friend, to whom he told all his troubles' (p.149). When he expostulates a little later that he would be proud and happy to have a 'genuine human friend' he is being very unfair, for she, as we can clearly see, is just that. Throughout what is effectively a long monologue she listens intently, makes him more tea, and gives him a cigarette. Her practical nature makes her most likeable, and she talks a great deal of sense in a few words. At times she laughs at his colourful, romantic diatribe, but she wisely lets him express all his problems.

An especially telling moment occurs when Tonio announces that he is 'not a nihilist'. Her reaction speaks volumes. She gulps over the phrase: 'She was lifting a tea-spoonful of tea to her mouth and paused in the act to stare at him.' (p.158). To her this is absurdly self-evident, and she is amazed at the mere suggestion. With real insight she lets him continue uninterrupted for three more pages in a 'Hamlet-like flow of oratory' (p.161). As she herself puts it, she listens 'faithfully'. When at last Tonio is 'expressed', and in a calmer mood is able to listen to her, she gently explains what to her has been obvious all along: that he is a bourgeois who does not realise it, or as she calls it, a 'bourgeois manqué'.

When next they meet, he announces his departure for the north. Her smile of satisfaction is that of a person who sees her friend on the road to recovery. When she asks for a letter about his experiences 'in—

Denmark' (p.162) the pause implies so much, for she really means 'in Lübeck': she knows he is going home and will rediscover his true nature. It is fitting that the Novelle ends with the promised letter. She deserves no less.

Irwin Immerthal

This unpleasant child suggests the damage that complacency can do to sensitive people. His father is president of the bank and significantly he also takes riding lessons, like Hans. Yet his physical appearance is almost a parody of Hans's beauty: 'His legs were crooked and his eyes were like slits.' (p.135). When he runs off, his malicious damage done: '. . . his eyes were only two gleaming cracks' (p.136); and he runs along the bench: '. . . with his crooked legs' (p.137).

The frank blue eyes and elastic tread that symbolise the lovely commonplace people are grotesquely distorted in Irwin; and this anticipates his childish meanness, when he mocks Tonio's foreign name. Irwin speaks: '. . . obviously intent to say just the right thing.' (p.136). His unthinking prejudice indicates the sort of bourgeois he will probably become. A society that contains adult Irwins in positions of authority urgently needs men like Tonio to point them to a higher set of values.

Francois Knaak

This 'unmentionable monkey' whose effects make no impression on his hardened colleague, Herr Heinzelmann, the pianist, is the embodiment of overpowering 'good form': 'How tranquil, how imperturbable was Herr Knaak's gaze! His eyes did not plumb the depths of things to the place where life becomes complex and melancholy; . . . To be able to walk like that, one must be stupid; then one was loved, then one was lovable.' (p.141). His name, his manners, his French all reek of artificiality. Certainly he plays the bourgeois at their own game and beats them, for most are too stupid to see through him. In brief he is a rather amusing fraud, harmless enough, but essentially one of the dilettanti whom Tonio despises. He is art without soul.

Years later Tonio sees his counterpart, a comic figure straight from a Danish novel, in his shiny boots, swallow-tail coat, and forever glancing at his bow of office. He places his feet 'in a very involved and artificial manner, toes first' (p.184). The elastic tread that symbolises the bourgeois is humorously exaggerated. This latter-day Knaak, officious as ever at the dance and speaking—'heaven save us!'—in French, brings back painful memories. Such men, though, are not true artists; they are really bourgeois playing at art in the dance of life. Tonio can never enjoy such trivial triumphs, for his art has a far loftier aim.

The Hamburg merchant

The entertaining incident with the would-be poet, like everything in the Novelle, is no mere coincidence. It is artistically foreshadowed by Tonio's story to Lisabeta of the Lieutenant who was foolish enough to read his verses in company: 'There he stood, suffering embarrassment for the mistake of thinking that one may pluck a single leaf from the laurel tree of art without paying for it with his life.' (p.161). His uniform and bearing and the polite dinner party are as much part of the formal bourgeois world as the Hamburger's business interests. The merchant's red-blond hair and red eyes are a comic distortion, thanks to the combination of lobster and the sea, of the bourgeois ideal of gold and blue. When the merchant gazes at the firmament and exclaims, 'we are worbs', Tonio is sure that 'he has no literature in his belly', merely lobster omelette! Yet Tonio's reaction is striking. In the presence of the Lieutenant he had felt guilt and pity; now he is merely amused and is 'privately drawn' to his 'engaging artlessness' (p.175). This is the new Tonio, one who loves all mankind.

Delightfully paralleling the earlier episode, next morning the merchant 'blushed rosy red for shame of the poetic indiscretions he had betrayed in the dark', and calls out a 'brisk and soldierly good-morning' (p.176)—we are back in the militarily precise world from which the lieutenant likewise should not have strayed!

The minor characters

Tonio reminisces about the criminal banker who wrote stories; about the morbidly self-conscious, unstable actor he once knew; about the poetic lieutenant; and about his friend Adalbert in the café, unable to cope with the seductions of real life. These are artists who reflect his own tendencies, and they live in the Novelle through the medium of Tonio's mind. However, the majority of the minor characters who flit briefly through the story are solid representatives of the Bürger class, honest, downright citizens who get on and live without asking too many questions and with a fundamental suspicion of artistic types.

The porter and the gentleman in black, Herr Seehaase, and Petersen, the policeman, all react to him in the same way. When at last Tonio escapes, accompanied by apologetic and respectful bows, the proprietor remarks: 'I told him at once he was on the wrong track . . .'. Tonio's 'Indeed!' is heavily ironic, for he knows he will never really belong fully to his father's class (p.172). The reaction of the library clerks had already rubbed in the fact, and at the Danish dance again everyone looks curiously and distrustfully at the stranger.

They themselves simply get on with the dance of life. Ferdinand

Matthiessen, for instance, tripping hand in hand with Inge at the dancing-class, is one of many red-headed revellers in the story. Their hair suggests as a leitmotif a humbler, less beautiful form of Hans's and Inge's type. The merchant has red hair. So do the American children in Aalsgaard. Their tutor and they exemplify an empty-headed existence. Whilst the landlady twitters and the apopletic fish-dealer snorts, they talk of sausage and the weather. All day long the tutor plays football with his charges: '. . . who had narrow, taciturn faces and reddish-yellow hair parted in the middle' (p.178). Even the parting in the middle becomes a feature of the story, for Tonio's bourgeois upbringing causes him to comb his hair with equal care. As life floods in on Tonio, so does the number of hotel guests increase: 'Quantities of people sitting at little tables enjoying beer and sandwiches amid lively discourse. There were whole families, there were old and young, there were even a few children.' (p.180). Yet as Tonio creeps back to his lonely room the story comes full circle, and we recall the character with whom he perhaps most identifies, Don Carlos, weeping because '. . . he is always so alone, nobody loves him.' (p.135).

The language

The imagery

'To see things clearly, if even through your tears, to recognise, notice, observe—and have to put it all down with a smile': this is the task demanded of the artist who wishes to order and shape 'a world unborn and formless'. Mann himself shows that it can be done. Quite apart from the symbolism of his leitmotifs, his story is studded with remarkable images, each capturing a mood, a gesture or a scene as exactly as the instantaneous photography in Hans's book of horses. Moreover, since Mann relates everything from Tonio's point of view, the accumulative effect of so many precise observations is to suggest that Tonio himself is an uncannily acute spectator at the dance of life. Thus the imagery becomes more than the mere colour on the canvas of Tonio's career; it reflects the very process of artistic creation that is at once his weakness and his strength.

Not surprisingly, therefore, many of the metaphors relate to art itself, reinforcing still further the egocentricity of the artist eternally isolated from the subject-matter of his art. Tonio's face matures with experience, for instance: 'the chiselled southern features were sharpened as though they had been gone over again with a graver's tool.' (p.150). The imagery, drawn from sculpture and engraving, emphasises at this meeting of a writer and a painter the brotherhood of art in its endless struggle with life. Soon music is involved to similar effect: 'We artists are all of us something like those unsexed papal singers . . . we sing like angels, but . . .' (p.153). The beauty of the castrato's voice is won at the cost of his physical enjoyment of life.

The prince and the actor parallel the lonely superiority of the artist and share his feelings: 'The sense of being set apart and not belonging, of being known and observed: something both regal and incongruous shows in the face.' (p.154). This hints at the frown on Tonio's forehead, the mark of Cain that symbolises the artist divorced from respectable life. The criminal banker and Tonio's near arrest pursue the theme. No. wonder he calls the artist 'a vain and frigid charlatan' (p.158), who hides behind 'his mask' (p.166), whilst his art is reduced to 'the sickly aristocracy of letters' (p.159), suggesting that, however aloof and inspired, the artist is fundamentally unhealthy. Indeed, Tonio is: 'half worn out by the fevers and frosts of creation.' (p.189). Here art is seen in terms of diseased and destructive nature, of extremes of heat and cold, reflecting the searing lust and icy intellect that make him a great artist, but a dissatisfied one who still seeks his justification. By contrast the rosy cheeks and healthy appetites of the Germans and Danes form a recurrent symbol of normal life, and the sunny weather reflects their happy, temperate mood.

Perhaps the most telling image of all occurs in Tonio's bitter-sweet musings at the hotel, when the latter-day Hans and Inge dance cheerfully past him: '. . . and yet to be forced to dance, dance the cruel and perilous sword-dance of art.' (p.187). Throughout the book the dance has symbolised the unthinking, unconcerned whirl of events that make up the happy-go-lucky lives of ordinary folk. The sword-dance is far more subtle and demanding than the boisterous romps in the hotel, or even the elegant quadrilles led by Monsieur Knaak. It requires just as much skill and control, and a slip can cause a serious wound. The essential difference, though, is simply this: the dancer is on his own. He performs for others, but only he can 'fall down in the dance'. The image perfectly matches Tonio's loneliness, his artistry and his sense of the cruel obligation to pursue his calling.

Yet the compensations are rich. Tonio eventually sees that his art can fruitfully serve his less-gifted fellows, and the sun bursts forth to symbolise his new-found joy and purpose. The fresh sunshine of a spring day in Lisabeta's work-room does much to help him see that there is more to life than mere 'fixative', mere abstract art. In his hotel room in Denmark, a brilliant sunrise heralds the new confidence that he feels: 'but now the sky was like a piece of pale-blue silk, spanned shimmering above sea and land and shot with light from red and golden clouds. The sun's disk rose in splendour from a crisply glittering sea that seemed to quiver and burn beneath it.' (p.180). The glorious freshness, colour and movement are felicitously evoked by the image of the piece of silk, for the material is beautifully flimsy and the light dances across it.

Even so, Tonio is still not part of the normal world he is now happy to serve, and in the Novelle he never becomes part of it. Such perfect harmony, where a purposeful artist would serve those he loved and who loved him, must remain for Tonio an ideal, a dream. The sea, beyond space and time, symbolises this yearning. Inevitably, then, many of Mann's loveliest phrases describe the sea. In them we witness the artist as he observes eternity.

It is no doubt stretching the point to derive from Mann's love of the sea the early image of the pupils 'rowing, right arm against the wind, towards dinner' (p.127), though it vividly conveys their struggle against the hail. Other expressions, though, beautifully catch the sea in its every mood. For example: 'the moon swam up with a silver gleam' (p.173) suggests the wiggling motion of the pale moonlight on the approaching waves, and the gentle sounds harmonise with the serenity of the scene. In complete contrast, Tonio's ship: 'glided down a steep mountain of a wave and her screw vibrated in agony.' (p.175). Here the mountains anticipate the 'foaming valleys, palely green' (p.179), lending to the wild picture the tone of Isaiah's awesome promises in the Bible, as nature is turned upside down and the propeller howls round in empty space behind the plunging vessel.

The 'unformed world' that the sea depicts in Tonio's mind (p.191) comes savagely to life: '. . . the water was lashed, torn and troubled; leaped upwards like great licking flames; hung in jagged and fantastic shapes above dizzy abysses . . .' (p.175). The consonants spit their fury. Every detail suggests destruction, a ripping and a burning. Like the clauses themselves, the sea leaps abruptly to a renewed climax. Even the momentous pause of the waves precedes their crashing back again. They claw upwards irrationally like flames, white against the dark sea. The brain reels before such violence, and most powerfully Mann thus implies the task confronting the artist. It is as daunting as Mann's own attempt in *Doktor Faustus* to give Germany back a sense of order amidst the chaos created by the Nazis.

The same elemental force intoxicates Tonio as he stands on the beach: 'The waves lowered their heads like bulls and charged against the beach . . .' (p.179). The curving menace of the bull's hunched neck is mirrored in the unfurling waves. Equally vivid, though aurally rather than visually this time, is the description of the sound of the surf: '. . . a noise like boards collapsing at a distance.' (p.179). Here the sound of the consonants matches the evocation of the echoing clap of the breaking waves scudding over the beach.

Yet Tonio is not content to emulate the sea in its more violent moods. After all, he is no maniacal Caesar Borgia. He may admire 'great and daemonic beauty' (p.190) but does not 'envy it'. His task is more positive: it is to redeem the confused world, and to give shape to the formlessness symbolised by the raging sea. In a gentler mood, the sea whispers to him its encouragement: '. . . and in his face the pure, fresh breath of the softly breathing sea' (p.179); 'And when the cold foam splashed his face it seemed in his half-dreams like a caress.' (p.176).

The breath on his cheek and the tender kiss now speak of love, anticipating the conclusion of the Novelle. For Tonio notices that amidst the tossing sea: 'above the spot where the sun hung behind the cloud a patch like white velvet lay on the sea.' (p.179). The misty velvet-like patch recalls the images of the pale-blue silk. Soon the sun will blaze forth on artistic and commonplace alike, and Tonio will fulfil his promise to Lisabeta.

'The pure chaste flame of his love' had seemed to go out on 'the sacrificial altar' (p.145). In fact, though, it has been burning darkly 'beneath the ashes of his fatigue' (p.164). 'The threads that bound him to his native city' (p.146) have been pulled taut again. At last Tonio can use the magic of his art to 'weave his spells' and redeem those he loves.

The leitmotif

Tonio speaks of 'the most miraculous case of all . . . the most typical, and therefore the most powerful of artists . . .' (p.155). From his reference to *Tristan and Isolde* he clearly means Richard Wagner. Thus Mann pays conscious tribute to the artist who in music has most vividly made use of leitmotif. In Part 4 we will trace Mann's similar technique in the literary sphere. Certainly his intention is to emulate the atmosphere that Wagner thereby achieves. Through constant repetition, our minds associate a physical detail with an emotion; and later we have only to read of the material object and the corresponding emotion will flood back in its wake.

This creates a hauntingly musical effect. The themes of art and life intertwine in the story, just as those of life and death echo through Wagner's opera; they lend artistic shape to the story. They reinforce the lesson that Tonio learns, for his aristry and his humanity require each other, if either is to flourish.

Inevitably, then, a sense of order emerges from the story. The formal pattern of the leitmotifs, that Tonio continually observes, subconsciously imbues him with the will to impose a similar discipline upon a world 'unborn and formless'. Not for him the daemonic self-indulgence of Caesar Borgia: Tristan and Isolde may end their lives in delirious, orgiastic nihilism, but Tonio takes an altogether more healthy and fruitful attitude.

Nietzsche had recognised in man two forces, the Dionysiac (after

Dionysus, Greek god of fertility and wine) and Apollonian (after Apollo, the Greek god of medicine, music and poetry). Dionysus stood for wild, uncontrolled passion; Apollo for classical, calm control. Tonio rejects the Wagnerian urge towards the Dionysiac in favour of the Apollonian. His artistic intellect seeks to create form from chaos. The leitmotif, perhaps more than any other feature of the Novelle, proves that Tonio's task is feasible.

It is not surprising that each material object evokes an emotional response. Tonio notices every physical detail of all he sees, and at the same time is uncomfortably aware of his own attendant feelings. Thus any recurrent symbol springs from Tonio's innermost being. Everyone he meets becomes a walking symbol of an attitude to life. Blond hair, blue eyes, an elastic stride, a neat parting, formal attire, and crisp German or Danish names are all immediately indicative of the dignified, courteous, uncomplicated bourgeoisie. Their cheerful dances, their healthy diet, even the prosaic sponge cake that Hans's reincarnation munches at the party all underline their 'carefree, happy companionship' (p.183). The smell of spring, and the sunshine streaming through an open window contrast strikingly with the smell of fixative and the closed windows at which Tonio tends to brood. Symbolically, too, the open window in the studio faces north, where Tonio's home lies.

At other times the seductive appeal of the south predominates. The dark complexion, hair and eyes, the clumsy gait, the frown or 'sign on the brow', the exotic names all bespeak those who are doomed to fall down in the dance. The bohemian freedom of the gypsies in their green wagon calls to Tonio, and we remember the unhappy, unloved little boy: 'The fountain, the old walnut tree, his fiddle, and away in the distance the North Sea, within sound of whose summer murmurings he spent his holidays—these were the things he loved, within these he enfolded his spirit, among these things his inner life took its course.' (p.132). Whether the tepid air of art or the sea breezes of life temporarily predominate, Tonio never loses his love of these earliest and most loyal companions.

The sword dance of art sets his misery in sharp relief against the recurring image of the happy dance of life. How often, we wonder, will Tonio again stand in the dark, taking a 'thievish pleasure' as he spies on dancers in the light? And so often he observes life from behind glass doors: his world is a framed picture, beautiful to behold, impossible to enter.

So much of his life is a quest for the 'right path'. This key image exactly mirrors his symbolic journeys to the south and to the north. Even as a child Tonio tends to 'get up and go away' from life. He asks Lisabeta 'What more pitiable sight is there than life led astray by art?' (p.160).

Significantly, as his personal crisis draws to a climax in Lübeck, twice he wonders: 'Where was he going?' He scarcely knows. Gradually, though, the mists of art recede and his debt to his forbears shines through. He gazes at the windows of the homes of his childhood friends, and the leitmotif of the window summons forth ghosts of both love and loneliness; and at last his question is answered: 'Where did he go? Towards home.' (p.166).

Now the path from the 'far blue south' leads back to the sterner values of his father's family. He tells the official in the library: 'I shall soon find my way about' (p.168) and symbolically he will soon be reconciled to his lot. Even so, he knows that much suffering will ensue: 'For some go of necessity astray, because for them there is no such thing as a right path.' (p.185). This brings us straight back to his adolescent conviction that '. . . he bore within himself the possibility of a thousand ways of life, together with the private conviction that they were all sheer impossibilities.' (p.146).

Tonio's way leads both to creation and to isolation. The image persists to the end, as he creeps down to the dance: 'He took this route, softly and stealthily as though on forbidden paths, feeling along through the dark, relentlessly drawn by this stupid jigging music . . .' (p.183). Even now that he can look objectively both at his loneliness and his artistic achievement, he still feels that in some way the artist remains a furtive, suspicious creature.

At last, then, Tonio can accept his mission in life, with all its joy and pain. He knows his life as an artist is not in vain. He knows too that he can never belong to the happy, simple folk he loves. Yet there remains for Tonio the consoling vision of an ideal world, in which form and shapelessness, art and life, indeed all the contradictions of his existence will be harmonised in sweet oblivion. Of this the symbol is the sea. It is a blissful reconciliation of all the forces in nature, both violent and mild. As a child Tonio has loved the 'strange and mysterious changes that whisk over the face of the sea' (p.134). As an adult on the boat to Denmark he gazes on the wild beauty of the waves. In a brief, pregnant sentence Mann instills into the sea all the vitality of human life: 'The sea danced' (p.175). Whether it leaps in a storm with flames of foam, or sparkles brilliantly beneath the sun on a 'rare and festal day', it symbolises eternity. Tonio feels 'in his face the pure, fresh breath of the softly breathing sea' (p.179). As he writes, it whispers to him, and with closed eyes he can see a world in need of order and redemption (p.191).

Inland, sitting beside a tree, Tonio gazes at the sea some way off— for life goes on, and the ideal remains remote: 'He held a book on his knee, but did not read a line.' (p.179). In the sight of eternity, even literature pales into insignificance: 'He enjoyed profound forgetfulness, hovered disembodied above space and time . . .' (p.179). One day, far off, all the pain and the longing, the envy, the contempt and the bliss will dissolve in the peace of the infinite. Meantime, the struggle for Tonio goes on. From his painful labours great works of art will be born. Their objectivity and form, exemplified by the leitmotifs in this Novelle, will help the inarticulate to understand, fashion, and enrich their lives.

The structure

The Novelle is perfectly symmetrical. Every character, as we have seen, effectively reappears and thus establishes a shape in Tonio's life. Similarly the leitmotifs weave a consistent pattern throughout the book. The incidents of childhood are relived in the light of Tonio's more mature and balanced outlook, when he is an experienced man. The twin poles of art and life, of south and north, revolve around a permanent focal point in Tonio himself. Through his eyes each event is observed, digested and elevated to a general philosophical statement. Everything then exemplifies Tonio's avowed intention to give form and meaning to his life and consequently to all life. As Mann says in *Die Forderung des Tages* (p.381): 'Form, endowed with the blessings of life, mediates between extremes of death—between death as formlessness and death as hyper-form, between disintegration and rigidity, coldness and ossification'— that is to say, between art like Adalbert's, existing for its own sake in a vacuum of no use to mankind, and an equally useless formal society, for whom convention and tradition have replaced warmth and energy. Mann concludes: 'Form is moderation and the measure of value, form is humanity, form is love.' The shape of the Novelle is, then, itself an indication of its message.

Conclusion

Through *Tonio Kröger* Thomas Mann has demonstrated his view that 'the artist is classless in a world divided into classes and engaged in a bitter class struggle'. In *Die Forderung des Tages* Mann argues that the artist is, therefore, 'mysteriously and uniquely the person in whom mankind can put his trust'. This is a reminder for which a world still torn apart by wars and jealousies can be grateful. In a society undermined by vested interests, we need men who can appraise people and ideas with cool, ironic detachment. The love of such men is the greater, in that they love what they see and yet do not seek to conceal its blemishes. Only from a truthful diagnosis can a cure be achieved. Today writers such as Böll* and Solzhenitsyn† bravely continue in Mann's path.

*Heinrich Böll (*b*.1917), the German novelist who won the Nobel Prize for Literature in 1972. His work satirises the heartless greed of contemporary society.
†Aleksandr Solzhenitsyn (*b*.1918), the Russian writer who won the Nobel Prize for Literature in 1970. He was expelled from the USSR in 1974 because his writings courageously exposed the true nature of the Communist system.

The book survives on a personal plane as well. The conflict between the artistic and bourgeois temperament may not be the problem of the majority of people. It never was. Yet the world remains as troubled as ever. The generation gap, the permissive society, to say nothing of the great questions of a nuclear age, give young and old quite enough problems of their own. People still seek as earnestly as Tonio a sense of spiritual and physical security. His confusion, hopes, fears, ideals, disillusionment, envy, contempt, bliss, above all his love of men and of the truth, are eternally ours to share.

Part 4

Hints for study

Points for detailed study

Tonio Kröger appeals immediately to most readers, for very few will share the bland, unthinking confidence of a Hans or an Inge. Most will, at some stage in their lives, feel a sense of inadequacy and yearn for the unattainable. Even those as composed and beautiful as the fair-haired, blue-eyed élite whom Tonio envies will perhaps eventually look at their more intellectual acquaintances and wonder whether their own lives are truly fulfilled. We identify very closely with Tonio, and since we suffer so keenly with him in his early despair, we can appreciate the power of his love at the end of the story. Though he remains estranged from the simple world, his life takes on a new sense of purpose, imbued with acceptance and charity.

When you analyse the Novelle, therefore, it is essential never to lose sight of this first, almost instinctive, identification with Tonio. Intellectual and artistic though they are, the ideas and effects of the story all stem from our initial sympathy with the troubled adolescent and the 'bourgeois manqué'.

Your primary task is, therefore, to examine Tonio's reaction to each event. Everyone he meets evokes a response in him, whether favourable or scornful, and helps him gradually to reconcile the conflict in his heart and mind. From this you can clearly show the themes of the story. You should trace the emotional and intellectual development of an agonised child into a purposeful, if still isolated, man. Intimately linked to this is, of course, the famous conflict of the Artist and the Man, which likewise is resolved when Tonio sees that his bourgeois and artistic tendencies can combine within him and enable him to produce art that will help the common man. Finally, the story traces the theme of artistic creation itself. You should show how Tonio analyses all he sees, and even from his own suffering deduces general truths about the nature of suffering. That is to say, he puts into words his own state of confusion. He helps others to look at his life and at their own lives and to draw a pattern from them.

Because we have identified so closely with Tonio, we realise how crucial this conclusion is to him. We can most easily illustrate Tonio's ambition to give shape to his fellows' lives by looking at Thomas

Mann's own life. Admittedly, Thomas Mann did briefly maintain that Hans Hansen's unthinking attitude was the correct one, when he was defending Germany's militarism in the First World War. He soon abandoned such narrow patriotism, though, and afterwards his every utterance was an appeal to moderation and to reason. In the mindless confusion wrought by the Nazis, Mann urged Germany to stop and think about what was happening. His intellect wove together the threads of the tattered nation and helped to restore sanity and democracy to a people who did not always accept him, but whom he loved. Like Tonio, he sought to give shape and meaning to the lives of those who were unable or unwilling to look beyond superficial gratification. People like Hans and Inge became putty in Hitler's hands, and it required artists such as the Mann brothers to wrest the putty back and to give it a finer shape.

Since the Novelle is a work of art about art, not surprisingly Mann's artistry blends inextricably with his ideas. You should show how gradually Tonio manages to give shape to his impressions and thus to his whole life. The structure and the style of the story perfectly reflect his development.

When you examine the structure, you should emphasise the beautiful symmetry. Every event in Tonio's youth is echoed as in a dream when he returns to the north; every character reappears in a slightly different guise. At the turning-point of the Novelle, his talk with Lisabeta, Tonio exorcises his earlier sense of helplessness. Now he knows that his art stems in part at least from his bourgeois origins, and he can use it to help his less artistic fellows. He feels a new sense of purpose and of love, and this is reflected in the harmony suggested by the balance of each section, each conversation, each character and each image.

The imagery matters greatly. What starts as a description echoes hauntingly throughout the story as a leitmotif. Tonio's individual problems take on a sense of permanence, and instead of *an* artist in one small society we see the problem of *the* artist in society. You will obviously want to trace this almost musical development of the images through the story and to underline the atmosphere and emotion that each one recalls. More personally, though, each will recall something for you and you alone, and you will see how *Tonio Kröger* is a different book for every reader. It strikes so personal a note that its universal appeal is paradoxically different in every case. Tonio is each of us, seeking to shape our lives as best we can.

This we can best do if we look honestly at ourselves, and this is the example that Tonio sets us. Even in his misery he can still see the other man's point of view, whether that of Knaak, the hotel manager, or Hans. However troubled, he still looks objectively at himself and draws general conclusions from his personal predicament. Such clear-sightedness gives him the strength to love and to create, even when he remains cut off from society. Again, Mann's style plays a crucial part in this.

His irony permeates the Novelle. It is easy to show the gentle contempt both Mann and Tonio feel for charlatans like Knaak, for his name and every gesture hint at the fraud beneath the pseudo-French exterior. At a more serious level, it is ironic that the young artist feels his calling to be almost a crime, and so he really rather approves of his own near arrest. Yet the supreme irony is that all along, the gypsy in Tonio owes his strength and love to those very middle-class values that he has sought to shun. The irony of the situation is always enhanced by phrases such as 'to a certain extent', emphasising Tonio's own uncertainy as he stands 'between two worlds' and 'at home in neither'. The ironic style, then, helps us and Tonio to see things thoughtfully. He can look dispassionately at his own passion and from his misery draw fruitful conclusions.

Thus at the end of the story Tonio, though still not happy in the way he would wish to be, enjoys a different sort of happiness, for he knows now that his life is not in vain. It is a most happy irony that he should end his letter to Lisabeta with virtually the same words that Mann used to describe the confused little boy who has just left his beloved Hans. The child has come to terms with the longing, the envy, the contempt and the bliss. Now the man knows his love is good and fruitful. He can use his creator's own words, for he has learned to look objectively at his problems and to draw inspiration from them.

Specimen questions

The three questions that follow illustrate the kind of topic that will interest both the appreciative reader of the story, and an examiner. They deal firstly with a principal feature of the language and structure—that is to say, the leitmotif; secondly, with a brief passage for detailed discussion, an exercise that sheds a surprising amount of light on the entire work; and finally, with a provocative generalisation about the nature of literature, which may or may not be true of *Tonio Kröger*. Each question emphasises particular features of the story, and so it is essential that quotations should not be random, but relevant.

---

(1) Analyse the use of leitmotif in *Tonio Kröger*

Nothing in *Tonio Kröger* is fortuitous. We have seen how Mann constantly quotes from an earlier passage of the story to awaken memories of an earlier mood. As Erich Heller says 'the leitmotif is a tidy symbol for the significantly ordered life',* and this is precisely what Tonio is

*The Ironic German, Secker and Warburg, London, 1958, p.72.

seeking. It is, therefore, upon the leitmotif that your own quotations should concentrate. Reflecting Mann's own technique, they should be brief and relevant.

You should trace the progress of a phrase through the story, for it will illustrate perfectly the way that Tonio himself comes to self-knowledge. At first a physical detail is associated with a spiritual or emotional quality. Once the link is firmly established in the reader's mind, he cannot see the physical detail again without its conjuring up the corresponding emotion. The more examples of this you can find, the more you will appreciate Mann's skill. What begins as an individual trait in one of Tonio's acquaintances ends as a characteristic feature of a whole type of people, and Tonio—and we—can therefore stand back from the subjective pangs of an emotion, and look objectively at the emotion itself. To look in this way is to judge, and to judge is to give a pattern to life.

An example of this technique occurs in our first sight of Tonio. We learn that, unlike Hans with his 'keen, far-apart, steel blue eyes', the little boy who gazes dreamily and timorously on the world has 'dark eyes, with delicate shadows and too heavy lids' (p.130). Thus dark eyes are linked to a sensitive nature in contrast to the blue ones of the sunny, unthinking Hans and Inge.

When Tonio meets Magdalena we are told she has 'great dark, brilliant eyes, so serious and adoring. She often fell down in the dance . . .' (p.141). Again dark eyes belong to those who worship poetry but cannot cope in the dance of everyday life. A little later Tonio laments that when he is famous:

'Magdalena Vermehren, who was always falling in the dances, yes, she would be impressed. But never Ingeborg Holm, never blue-eyed, laughing Inge. So what was the good of it?' (p.144)

Here the dark eyes are recalled by contrast with the blue, and Magdalena's kinship in suffering again links her to Tonio. Much later in Denmark he sees the reincarnation of this unhappy child. The pale, awkward girl with the bitter mouth sits all alone at the dance: ' . . . her head was drooped, yet she was looking at Tonio Kröger with black, swimming eyes. He turned away . . . ' (p.186). The drooping head recalls Tonio's own habit of tilting his head to one side, and the black eyes now firmly establish the Danish girl as another of those clumsy, sensitive people who find normal daily life beyond them. We know she will fall down in the dance, for like Magdalena and Tonio, she should remain behind glass doors, as one of life's spectators. When he helps her to her feet and bids her dance no more, the 'dark, swimming eyes' with which she gazes at him recall a whole lifetime's loneliness and aspirations in Tonio himself.

So much, then, can be conveyed in those words 'dark eyes'. Of course Mann is not saying that in real life the blue-eyed must win and the others fail. He is saying that a certain type of person, here symbolised by the epithet 'dark eyed', will find life too much for them; unless, like Tonio, they learn to harmonise all the tendencies in their souls. The eyes vividly call attention to the problem.

This symbolic use of leitmotif suits Mann's ironic style. Everything seems so predictable that we can only pity those who try to defy their own natures. Sometimes the irony is heavily sarcastic, sometimes gentle, sometimes cheerful, but always it reminds us of the division in Tonio's heart. You should pick out examples of Mann's irony. The hilarious conversation on the deck at night well illustrates, for instance, the dangers to a good, sound citizen of moments of poetic inspiration! No wonder the Hamburg businessman 'studiously avoided him' after his indiscretions of the previous evening. Yet much more subtle are the frequent notes of hesitation that flit through the text, hinting at Tonio's deep sense of guilt and doubt all the time that he cannot reconcile his art with everyday life. When, for example, his mother swiftly remarries a musician with an Italian name and goes off into 'remote blue distances' —so typical of the gypsy side of Tonio's nature—he finds it 'rather irregular', for his father's influence is clearly at work here. Yet Mann adds: '. . . but who was he to call her to order, who wrote poetry himself and could not even give an answer when asked what he meant to do in life?' (p.146).

Once more we see Tonio desperately apologetic and unsure of himself. As long as Tonio remains like this, Mann makes him qualify all his opinions, and you should look for other illustrations of this technique. As Professor Wilkinson says, his gentle irony is ideal for a situation 'in which the artist admires and needs the Bürger and the Bürger replies by arresting him!'*

---

(2) Write a critical commentary on a chosen passage from *Tonio Kröger*

It is often helpful to analyse a specific passage from the text, always relating it to the work as a whole. Even if you are not required in an examination to write a critical appreciation it remains a demanding exercise which succinctly illustrates many of the finer points of the story. You might, for instance, select this passage for your commentary:

'And his father too had drawn his last breath in the same room: that tall, correct, slightly melancholy and pensive gentleman with the wild flower in his buttonhole. . . . Tonio had sat at the foot of his death-bed, quite given over to unutterable feelings of love and grief. His

Tonio Kröger, Oxford, 1968, p.xxxvi.

mother had knelt at the bedside, his lovely, fiery mother, dissolved in
hot tears; and after that she had withdrawn with her artist into the
far blue south. . . . And beyond still, the small third room, likewise
full of books and presided over by a shabby man—that had been for
years on end his own. Thither he had come after school and a walk—
like today's; against that wall his table had stood with the drawer
where he had kept his first clumsy heart-felt attempts at verse. . . .
The walnut tree . . . a pang went through him. He gave a side-wise
glance out at the window. The garden lay desolate, but there stood
the old walnut tree where it used to stand, groaning and creaking
heavily in the wind. And Tonio Kröger let his gaze fall upon the book
he had in his hands, an excellent piece of work, and very familiar.
He followed the black lines of print, the paragraphs, the flow of words
that flowed with so much art, mounting in the ardour of creation to
a certain climax and effect and then as artfully breaking off. . . .
  "Yes, that was well done," he said; put back the book and turned
away. Then he saw that the functionary still stood bolt-upright,
blinking with a mingled expression of zeal and misgiving.' (p.168).

When you write a critical appreciation you should immediately state
the context of the passage. The position will often be significant, and in
this case is crucial. After his discussion with Lisabeta, Tonio returns to
his home town. He is no longer the bitterly disillusioned child at the
start of the story. Now, in a mood of thoughtful reconciliation, he can
see the debt that he owes his father and his home town. Their middle-
class northern values, he now realises, have played and will continue to
play a fruitful and necessary part in his life as an artist. Thus this passage
poignantly recalls memories of earlier ones. So much is similar, and yet
how much has changed! As in a dream Tonio relives his youth, but
now the emotional atmosphere is one of respectful gratitude. The nightmare of adolescence at last behind him, he can now go on to Denmark.
The problem of the isolated artist will remain, but he will at least be able
to face it and make something constructive of it. This passage shows us
in practical terms, then, that Tonio's conversation with Lisabeta really
was the turning-point in his life.

Next, you should decide upon the main theme of your chosen passage.
If it is well written, every detail will in some way relate to this central
idea; if not, some phrases will be exposed as mere padding. This theme
should in turn be harnessed to the main idea of the work as a whole;
such concentric circles display the artistic unity of the Novelle. The
essential theme of *Tonio Kröger* is the hero's struggle to reconcile the
conflicting pulls of 'art' and 'normal life' within him. The conversation
with Lisabeta, for example, tends to concentrate on the first half of the
conflict, whereas the cheerful party in the hotel emphasises the other

side. In any scene, though, the central problem is the focal idea. In our passage, Mann brilliantly blends the worlds of the artist and the citizen. Here the twin pulls of the conflict have achieved stability. Through the eyes of the eternal spectator, Tonio, we see the home that has become the public library. Life has bred art, which returns to the people, who will use the books to improve their lives. This scene, then, proves that art and life belong together. Though Tonio will remain lonely, his art will not be pointless; it will serve life. This passage, then, exactly mirrors the theme of the whole story.

This introduction to your commentary should be very precise. Do not waste time retelling the plot, for the reader, probably an examiner, knows that well enough. State the context briefly, elucidate the themes concisely, and concentrate on explaining the significance of each statement you make. It is pointless, for instance, just to observe that Mann describes Tonio revisiting his home which has now become a library. Anyone can see that for himself. Your task is to say *why* and *how* he describes the visit. You must examine the symbolism of the Library and of the many leitmotifs that echo through the passage. In other words, this is much more than a visit to a library. It is a vital stage in Tonio's development. It harmonises all the discordant notes in his past life and points the way to a constructive future.

It is helpful also to mention the tone of the passage. There are moments of high comedy and moments of near desperation for 'the tragic and laughable figures' that Tonio himself, like Mann, wishes to redeem. And all the time the author's gentle irony reminds us to emulate Tonio: to stand back and observe, 'to see things clear, if even through your tears.' Though we may hope to be more integrated into 'normal' life than Tonio, we need to learn something of his artistic objectivity. Only if we look clearly at the world do we have the right to make moral judgements about it. In our chosen passage Mann shows us everything through Tonio's eyes, and thus we share his pangs of nostalgia, his pride in creation, his sense of isolation. No matter how personal the memory it is faithfully and objectively recorded by Mann. Like the passage that Tonio recognises in his book, the words flow artistically, mount to a climax, and as artfully break off. 'Yes, that was well done', says Tonio, and we feel the same of this passage. Like Tonio in his dream-like state, we too can review his past life and see in it a pattern that will shape his future works. Here the whole passage is steeped in irony, for Tonio has at last learned that the paternal influence he sought to escape is an integral and positive force within his art.

Now you must explain the point of any detail that is worthy of comment. In our particular passage the actual words are easy enough to understand. At other times, however, a note of explanation will be necessary. When Tonio speaks of *Don Carlos*, for instance, you should explain that he is referring to Schiller's play. Much more to the point, though, you must also point out how the king, a lonely man, betrayed by his friend, seems to the young Tonio to be his literary twin soul. Always, then, show the full significance of a phase; and do it systematically. You might work steadily through the next, or if you prefer, pick out examples that relate to a particular theme. Many expressions, for instance, hauntingly recall similar, but not identical, earlier ones, and you could well consider all these leitmotifs together, for they all work towards the same effect.

Here, Tonio's father is once more recalled. The wild flower in his buttonhole has come to represent the formal virtues of the immaculate Bürger. Now, though, he is not just 'correct' but also 'slightly melancholy and pensive', and this new description implies a warmer sympathy for him and his values in Tonio's heart. As ever, after the father comes a mention of the mother. Her withdrawal with her new husband, an artist, to the 'far blue south' evokes memories of the libertine gypsy which have hitherto clashed with those of Consul Kröger. Now, though, the memory of both is symbolically linked in love, grief and hot tears at the bed-side. Other symbols flood through Tonio's mind: books; school; the walk with Hans; verse; the walnut-tree; art; and a suspicious public official, must all suggest to him what they suggest to us. Each summons up some aspect of the conflict that has torn him in two. Now the pieces are coming together again. As an artist, he will still be an object of suspicion to 'normal' folk; after all, only hours later he is all but arrested as a criminal on the run. Within himself, though, he is now at peace, and he can leave his home. It now serves the public, and he wishes to do the same.

As well as the imagery, other features of the style merit your attention. The near-repetition of the earlier phrases contributes to Tonio's dream-like sense of reliving his life; the tiny changes suggest that he has nevertheless matured. The rows of dots between the sentences and phrases tenderly reflect the motion of his eyes, and the consequent emotion in his heart. Slowly his gaze roves round the house and memories spring up with a pang. The wall recalls the table where he wrote his verses; this in turn reminds us (and him, no doubt) of Storm's *Immensee*, which he read as the walnut-tree groaned. We think also of Storm's lovely line, 'I would sleep but thou must dance', and thus we recall the lovely Inge and the lonely, aching misfit at the dance. This in turn artistically anticipates the dance in Denmark. Throughout runs the symbol of the dance of life. All this flits through out thoughts as we follow the dots between 'verse' and 'the walnut-tree'. Our identification with Tonio is strengthened by the style.

The artful climax of the paragraph so delicately matches the one that Tonio is admiring in his book, that he is satisfied and puts back the book and 'turns away'. This gesture anticipates his leaving the town, and recalls many other moments when Tonio 'goes his way'. This time, though, we feel that for this artist there is 'a right way' at last, for, with all his suffering, he now has a purpose. Suddenly the mood is broken, for Tonio realises that he is being watched with 'zeal and misgiving'. The abrupt and prosaic vocabulary of the sentence contrasts utterly with the elegant unfurling of the previous sentences, and again the style cleverly reflects the mood, as Tonio, reconciled to his past as he may be, is harshly reminded that as an artist he remains an outsider.

The tenses of the verbs are always revealing. Here the pluperfects of his youth make way for the simple past tense of his actions, as his gaze sweeps round the room. Imperceptibly Tonio's past and present have come together again, for they have always really been inseparable. Similarly you should carefully examine the type of vocabulary the author uses. The 'far blue south' and 'a certain climax' lend a hazy quality to the passage, suggesting an almost indefinable sense of beauty which contrasts strikingly with the simple physical details of the rest of the passage. This in turn suggests the twin poles of Tonio's vision—the physical world, and the symbolical significance that he deduces from his clinical observation. Thus, the smallest detail of the style contributes to our appreciation of the conflict between life and art.

In your final paragraph it would be useful to show how this passage is an integral part of the whole section. Tonio begins his journey north because he wishes to re-establish contact with simple healthy normality, and this whole section has a cathartic impact upon him. The visit to his home town finally lays the ghosts of his youth, and he can go on to Denmark and 'real life' as a useful artist. The scene in the library is the climax of his dream-like journey through the town. Every detail of his homecoming helps to build up this climax. His emotion contrasts strongly with the derision he had felt on leaving years ago; still he observes everything; still the fair, easy-going populace affect him. Memories seep back, and he dresses carefully, for his father's values are beginning to reassert themselves. The artist for once does not wish to use words, nor even to sign the register legibly. The 'son of the house' has returned to the home of his fathers. Within this house his father's mother had died after a long struggle, for she 'clung to life'. The life force is everywhere apparent. The old virtues of the 'Bürgertum' have never died in Tonio, and now the Public Library symbolically shows him how his art can serve the community. Meantime, the 'disdainful eye of the porter and the gentleman in black' in his hotel anticipate his near arrest at the end of the section. Suspicion of the artist will linger on; the dancers in Denmark in turn will eye him uneasily as he looks through the window; but Tonio can now enjoy life in his own way. His joke on the policeman is 'a little effect he had worked out to perfection'.

The artist can now lend shape to his own life and happily, as he predicted to Lisabeta, it may even 'turn out rather funny'.

---

(3) 'The great figures of modern literature come alive for us because their experience is rendered, not their appearance' (T.J. Reed). Discuss with reference to *Tonio Kröger*

Whichever essay you have to write, you must have a plan. Begin by analysing the title, for until you do, you run the risk of incoherence. Sometimes this will merely entail a quick definition of a word such as 'irony' or 'leitmotif'. At other times a statement may require careful elaboration. This is true of Dr Reed's observation* quoted in the above question. If your essay is not to ramble hopelessly, you must define your terms. What, for a start, is 'modern'? Decide whether by this you understand 'since the Romantic movement', 'this century', 'since the Second World War' or even more recently. (Dr Reed himself, in fact, illustrates his point with reference to Tolstoy.) When, moreover, does a literary figure merit the epithet 'great'? This word, so often abused in the daily papers, must apply only to truly exceptional creations. Knaak or Hans are not great, for they appear only briefly, and anyway are mere types who symbolise for Tonio an attitude to life. Tonio, himself, though, may well be 'great', for he lives vividly as a personality with whom we can all identify; he exists on both a human and an allegorical plane, he is *an* adolescent and *the* adolescent, *an* artist and *the* artist, *an* outsider and *the* outsider. State exactly what the word means to you, and your essay will have a framework worthy of its subject, for whom form means everything. Even the little word 'because' can be treacherous, for there is a hint that experience is 'therefore' more vivid than appearance. It is probably true, in fact, that the intimate emotions and reflections of a person tell us more of his character than his outward manners, behaviour and dress. It is certainly true that Mann uses external appearance artistically to create a leitmotif which will suggest a corresponding emotional or intellectual state. Appearance does matter, then, but is subordinated to experience.

Once you have thoroughly grasped the point of the question, and only then, you can follow the plan of your essay. Incidentally, notice that you are asked to refer to *Tonio Kröger* and not Tonio Kröger, in other words to the story and not just to the hero. In some cases this could be a crucial distinction. It would be true to say, for example, that Tonio Kröger is often confused, but quite false to describe as often confused so carefully planned a work as *Tonio Kröger*. Watch your inverted commas!

Your essay on the greatness of Tonio Kröger falls readily into two

*Thomas Mann—The Uses of Tradition, Clarendon Press, Oxford, 1974, p.58.

parts: firstly, those aspects of the story that render the experience of the characters; and secondly, those that render their appearance. You should illustrate their emotional development and their physical descriptions. The essay will be far more interesting, though, if you show at the outset how these two features combine to demonstrate the different calls of art and life. Fair hair and blue eyes are indeed physical attributes that form a major feature of the story, but Hans, Inge and the Danes emerge as representatives of a way of life rather than as individuals. The appearance of fair hair and blue eyes is essentially one aspect of the workings of Tonio's soul, of his emotional experience.

You should, then, relate all your observations to the essential problem of the story. In the same way, essays on topics as diverse as irony or symbolism will be much more persuasive if they follow a plan that not only neatly illustrates these techniques, but also underlines the division in Tonio's psyche. The principal sections of an essay should in turn be subdivided into more manageable sections. Essentially you want to bring out the meaning and the artistry of the work. To find the meaning, you need to examine the themes of the artist and society; of artistic creation; and of Tonio's development from bitter disillusion to fruitful reconciliation. To analyse the artistry you should examine the style of the language; the structure of the story; and the characterisation. You should notice, too, the blend of tragedy and comedy that attends Tonio's search for fulfilment. These sections can be subdivided for the sake of clarity. An obvious case, for instance, is the characterisation, where you might group those who belong to the 'commonplace' and those who belong to the sensitive, lonely, artistic world. Illustrate your points with quotations from the text.

There is no one answer to a literary essay. What matters is to be clear, and to justify what you say. A final paragraph can round off your essay, summing up the principal points and perhaps broadening its horizons. Tonio's experience, for instance, is a reminder to mankind of the need to face one's problems honestly and to seek order out of seeming chaos. You might therefore conclude that the standard-bearer of so relevant a theme deserves a place among the 'great figures of modern literature'.

Above all, like Tonio, be truthful. Sometimes an essay will be fairly straightforward. A character study of Knaak, for example, speaks for itself. Mann's humour debunks him thoroughly and shows the fraud beneath the superficial elegance, and you can easily show this. A more taxing essay, though, will ask you to comment on a provocative remark. Take, for example, T.E. Apter's declaration that Tonio shows 'an irritating narcissism'.* Certainly Tonio is aware of his fame as an artist, and feels 'a touch of contempt' for those he professes to love. Is he really, though, showing 'literary bad manners' and actually ridiculing

* *The Devil's Advocate*, Macmillan, London, 1978, p.31.

Hans and Inge? Again you should follow a systematic plan and illustrate the arguments for and against Mr Apter's view. You may agree with him, or you may feel that Tonio's problem is burningly real and stems from his fatal sense of being 'called to art' away from the world he yearns for. Your conclusion this time must depend on your personal opinion. Never be afraid to disagree with the statement in the title. Sift all the evidence and make up your own mind.

Further specimen questions

(a) 'Tonio's dilemma reflects the psychological insecurity of modern man'. Discuss.

(b) 'The story is essentially optimistic'. Discuss.

(c) What impression of the 'Bürger' and of the artist do you gain from the story?

(d) What is your own view of the artist's moral responsibilities? How far does it coincide with Tonio's?

(e) How convincing is the antithesis Tonio draws between life and art?

(f) To what extent can one say Tonio *is* Thomas Mann? Is the auto-biographical element relevant in evaluating the story?

(g) 'Mann's greatest achievement lies in his controlled and purposeful use of irony'. To what purpose does he put his irony here?

(h) Analyse the humour in the story.

(i) Discuss the symbolism in *Tonio Kröger*.

(j) Discuss the imagery in *Tonio Kröger*.

(k) Discuss the use of *leitmotif*.

(l) Discuss the characterisation.

(m) 'Tonio's humility disguises an intolerable arrogance'. Discuss.

(n) Does Tonio's personality develop in the course of the story?

(o) Discuss Mann's portrayal of adolescence.

(p) What is the symbolic value of the dances?

(q) What is the significance of Tonio's conversation with Lisabeta and of his letter to her?

(r) How vividly does Mann evoke the atmosphere of a locality, and for what symbolic end?

(s) Analyse the scene in which Tonio is nearly arrested.

(t) Why has Tonio's home become a Public Library?

(u) 'Literary ambition is revealed as a form of the Will to Power' (T.J. Reed). How far is Tonio imbued with Nietzsche's philosophy?

(v) What is the influence in the story of Wagner and Schopenhauer?

(w) Discuss the role of the Apollonian and the Dionysiac in the story.

(x) Analyse the structure of the story.

(y) How far is *Tonio Kröger* typical of the German Novelle?

(z) '*Tonio Kröger* is a poem in prose'. Discuss.

Part 5

Suggestions for further reading

The text

The story appears in German in the *Gesammelte Werke in zwölf Bänden*, Frankfurt am Main, 1960.

Two student editions are by: E.M. Wilkinson, Blackwell's German Texts, Blackwell, Oxford, 1944, reprinted 1968, which has a very useful introduction; and J.A. Kelly, Harrap, London, 1949, which has an introduction and vocabulary.

In English there is Mrs H.T. Lowe-Porter's sensitive translation, published by Secker & Warburg, London, 1928. This is available in the Penguin Modern Classics edition, entitled *Death in Venice; Tristan; Tonio Kröger*, Penguin Books, Harmondsworth, 1971; reprinted 1977, in association with Secker & Warburg. This translation of *Tonio Kröger* is available in the U.S.A. in *Stories of Three Decades*, Alfred A. Knopf, New York, first published 1936.

Other works by Thomas Mann

From the collected works, certain volumes are particularly helpful in appreciating *Tonio Kröger*.

(*i*) SHORT STORIES: *Tristan* (1902)
                Der Tod in Venedig (1913) (*Death in Venice*)
(*ii*) NOVELS: *Buddenbrooks* (1901) (English version, 1924)
               Der Zauberberg (1924) (*The Magic Mountain*, 1927)
               Doktor Faustus (1947) (*Doctor Faustus*, 1948)
These have all been translated by Mrs Lowe-Porter for Secker & Warburg, and are reissued in the Penguin Modern Classics, Penguin Books, Harmondsworth.

Biography

HANS BURGIN AND HANS OTTO MAYER (translated by Eugene Dobson): *Eine Chronik seines Lebens* (*A Chronicle of his Life*), University of Alabama Press, Alabama, 1969.

HAROLD NICHOLSON: *The Brothers Mann*, Secker & Warburg, London, 1979.

Criticism

From literally thousands of articles and books on Mann's thought and style the following are particularly helpful:

GEORG LUKACS (translated by S. Mitchell): *Essays on Thomas Mann*, Merlin Press, London, 1964.

ERICH HELLER: *The Ironic German*, Secker & Warburg, London, 1958.

T.J. REED: *Thomas Mann—The Uses of Tradition*, Clarendon Press, Oxford, 1974. (This is the most authoritative study in English on Thomas Mann.)

The Novelle

E.K. BENNETT (revised and continued by H.M. Waidson): *A History of the German Novelle*, Cambridge University Press, 1934; reprinted 1949.

The author of these notes

COLIN NIVEN was educated at Dulwich College and was an Exhibitioner in Modern Languages at Gonville and Caius College, Cambridge. Formerly a Housemaster at Fettes College, he is now Head of Modern Languages at Sherborne School. He is the author of the York Notes volume on Voltaire's *Candide*.

The first 150 titles

		Series number
ATHOL FUGARD	*Selected Plays*	(63)
MRS GASKELL	*North and South*	(60)
WILLIAM GOLDING	*Lord of the Flies*	(77)
OLIVER GOLDSMITH	*She Stoops to Conquer*	(71)
	The Vicar of Wakefield	(79)
THOMAS HARDY	*Jude the Obscure*	(6)
	Tess of the D'Urbervilles	(80)
	The Mayor of Casterbridge	(39)
	The Return of the Native	(20)
	The Trumpet Major	(74)
	Under the Greenwood Tree	(129)
L. P. HARTLEY	*The Go-Between*	(36)
	The Shrimp and the Anemone	(123)
NATHANIEL HAWTHORNE	*The Scarlet Letter*	(134)
ERNEST HEMINGWAY	*A Farewell to Arms*	(145)
	For Whom the Bell Tolls	(95)
	The Old Man and the Sea	(11)
HERMANN HESSE	*Steppenwolf*	(135)
ANTHONY HOPE	*The Prisoner of Zenda*	(88)
RICHARD HUGHES	*A High Wind in Jamaica*	(17)
THOMAS HUGHES	*Tom Brown's Schooldays*	(2)
HENRIK IBSEN	*A Doll's House*	(85)
	Ghosts	(131)
HENRY JAMES	*Daisy Miller*	(147)
	The Europeans	(120)
	The Portrait of a Lady	(117)
	The Turn of the Screw	(27)
SAMUEL JOHNSON	*Rasselas*	(137)
BEN JONSON	*The Alchemist*	(102)
	Volpone	(15)
RUDYARD KIPLING	*Kim*	(114)
D. H. LAWRENCE	*Sons and Lovers*	(24)
	The Rainbow	(59)
	Women in Love	(143)
HARPER LEE	*To Kill a Mocking-Bird*	(125)
CHRISTOPHER MARLOWE	*Doctor Faustus*	(127)
SOMERSET MAUGHAM	*Selected Short Stories*	(38)
HERMAN MELVILLE	*Billy Budd*	(10)
	Moby Dick	(126)
ARTHUR MILLER	*Death of a Salesman*	(32)
	The Crucible	(3)
JOHN MILTON	*Paradise Lost I & II*	(94)
	Paradise Lost IV & IX	(87)
SEAN O'CASEY	*Juno and the Paycock*	(112)
EUGENE O'NEILL	*Mourning Becomes Electra*	(130)
GEORGE ORWELL	*Animal Farm*	(37)
	Nineteen Eighty-four	(67)
JOHN OSBORNE	*Look Back in Anger*	(128)
HAROLD PINTER	*The Birthday Party*	(25)
	The Caretaker	(106)
THOMAS PYNCHON	*The Crying of Lot 49*	(148)